THE *art* OF OPTIONS TRADING IN AUSTRALIA

THE *art* OF OPTIONS TRADING IN AUSTRALIA

Christopher Tate

Wrightbooks

First published 2002 by Wrightbooks
an imprint of John Wiley & Sons Australia Ltd
42 McDougall Street Milton Q 4064
Offices also in Melbourne

Typeset in 11/13.2 pt California

Share price charts created with SuperCharts

© Christopher Tate 2002

The moral rights of the author have been asserted

Reprinted 2004 and 2007

National Library of Australia Cataloguing-in-Publication data

---

Tate, Christopher.
The art of options trading in Australia.

Includes index.
ISBN 0 7016 3732 3.

1. Stock options - Australia. 2. Stock warrants - Australia.
3. Derivative securities - Australia. I. Title.

332.63280994

Cover design by Rob Cowpe

Disclaimer
The material in this publication is of the nature of general comment only, and neither purports nor intends to be advice. Readers should not act on the basis of any matter in this publication without considering (and if appropriate, taking) professional advice with due regard to their own particular circumstances. The author and publisher expressly disclaim all and any liability to any person, whether a purchaser of this publication or not, in respect of anything and of the consequences of anything done or omitted to be done by any such person in reliance, whether whole or partial, upon the whole or any part of the contents of this publication.

Contents

Option Market Basics

Why do some market participants trade options?

The answer to this is quite easy: the Australian exchange-traded options market is one of the most dynamic, innovative and exciting of markets available and options themselves are one of the most profitable tools available to traders. Options are used by both large and small traders because of their leverage, risk management capability and capacity to greatly enhance the return on assets.

By the end of this chapter you should be able to:

- ▲ Distinguish between company-issued and exchange-traded options.
- ▲ Define the basic types of options.
- ▲ Define which options are bullish and which are bearish.
- ▲ Understand the components of an option.
- ▲ Understand basic option terminology.
- ▲ Understand the presentation of option quotes.
- ▲ Understand the six basic strategies and their payoff diagrams.

Exchange-Traded Options

Before we begin talking about exchange-traded options (ETOs) it is necessary to be able to distinguish between ETOs and company-issued options. Most traders are familiar with company-issued options. These are options issued by companies as a means of raising capital, and they are traded on the Australian Stock Exchange (ASX). They are generally 'European' in nature, which means they may only be exercised on the day of expiry. Upon exercise the number of shares on issue will rise as the options are converted to ordinary shares. It is this conversion to ordinary shares that enables companies to raise equity.

ETOs are not issued by the company, they are traded on the Australian Options Market (AOM), a subsidiary of the ASX. ETOs are known as 'American'-style options—they can be exercised at any time. The exercise of such options does not result in any change to the capital structure of the underlying company. ETOs fall into the class of securities known as 'derivatives'; their existence and price is derived from an underlying security, in this case an ordinary share.

It is here that I must issue my first warning about trading ETOs. If you cannot successfully trade shares then it will be almost impossible for you to trade any form of derivative. All derivatives trading will allow you to do is be more flamboyant in your failure.

As a share trader you should be able to answer the following questions with ease:

- What is your entry trigger? Do you believe this to be the secret of successful trading?
- What is your position sizing methodology?
- What is your exit strategy?
- What is the expectancy of your trading system?

If you cannot answer these questions then your chances of succeeding at options trading will be quite small. You will need to set yourself the task of learning about these facets of trading before you even consider a move into derivatives.

Options Basics

An ETO is the right but not the obligation to buy or sell a given security at a certain price within a given time. So if I purchase a BHP-Billiton call option I have bought the right but not the obligation to buy BHP-Billiton shares at a set price by a given time. As an example, if I have bought a BHP-Billiton July 1100 call, I have bought the right to buy BHP-Billiton shares at $11.00 on or before the expiry date in July. (You will notice that when I write $11.00, I write it as 1100; this is a form of shorthand that is used to describe the strike or exercise price of an option. So an NAB June 3650 call is an NAB $36.50 call option.)

Conversely, a put option is the right but not the obligation to sell a given security at a certain price within a given time. So if I purchase an NCP June 1000 put I have bought the right but not the obligation to sell News Corp at $10.00 on or before the end of June.

When an option is described there are four components that make up the description:

- the stock being traded (this is referred to as the underlying stock)
- the expiry date
- the strike or exercise price
- whether it is a put or a call option.

All option descriptions contain these four basic elements. This is how an order is conveyed to a broker. The components of an options contract are looked at later in this chapter.

When an option is purchased it has to be purchased from someone. It is important to note that there are two sides to an options transaction, and it is here that we run into our first piece of jargon. If I buy an option as an opening position I am said to be an *option buyer* or *option taker*. So if my instruction to my broker is to buy ten NAB July 3500 calls to open I am an option buyer. In performing this trade I am said to be long that particular option. The maximum potential loss for an option buyer is limited to the amount paid for the option. Option buyers are also said to have undertaken a debit transaction. It has cost this person money to initiate the position. This concept is extended when we look at spreads. Any spread that costs money to initiate is a debit spread.

If my instruction to my broker had been to sell ten NAB July 3500 calls to open then I have initiated a short options position and I am referred to as an *option writer* or an *option seller*. A trader who sells an option as an opening transaction is an option writer. The option writer receives a premium from the option buyer for that particular option. In the case of spreads, any spread that generates a credit is referred to as a credit spread.

A call option writer can be either covered or naked. A covered option writer will own the underlying shares against which the call option has been written. For example, a trader who owned 5,000 ANZ shares and then wrote five ANZ calls against this position would be referred to as a covered writer (an option contract generally gives the trader leverage over 1,000 shares). A trader who simply writes options without owning the underlying security is said to have taken on a naked position. Naked call option writers are liable for margins to be levied against their account by the ASX, and they will have to buy the shares on the market if the option is exercised.

Option writers are said to have undertaken a credit transaction since they receive an option premium when the position is initiated. In some instances, option writers can face theoretically unlimited losses.

It is very important that traders understand the differences between being an option buyer/taker and an option writer/seller. Each has a differing set of obligations and a different risk profile.

Option buyers/takers have the right but not the obligation to exercise their option; for this they pay a premium. This premium is the maximum amount they can lose. For example, if I had paid 35¢ for a given option then the most I can lose is 35¢ per share. I cannot lose any more than that.

Option writers/sellers are under a potential obligation to either deliver stock if they are call option writers or buy stock if they are put option writers. For this obligation they receive a premium from the option buyer. It is possible for an option writer to face a theoretically unlimited loss. This loss is only theoretically unlimited because a stock will eventually stop going up or down, but this is a rather moot point when you are faced with a position that is moving rapidly against you.

It is very important for option writers to understand their obligations and the potential for loss that such positions carry. To illustrate this, consider the following. If I write an NCP June 1200 put I am obligated to purchase NCP at $12.00 if the option buyer chooses to exercise the contract. (Remember there are two parts to the contract; there is the option writer and there is the option buyer.) The put option buyer has the right but not the obligation to sell NCP at $12.00 on or before the expiry date of the option.

My view in writing this put is that I believe NCP will go up. Option writers have the opposite view to option buyers. If I write a put option I am bullish, and the person buying it is bearish. It is always the buyer who has the right to exercise the contract.

Let's assume that my view of NCP is incorrect and NCP falls precipitously to $5.00 and the put option buyer exercises the right to sell NCP at $12.00, and I have the stock put to me. Irrespective of the price NCP is trading at in the market I have to pay $12.00. I now face a loss of $7.00 per share since I will be forced to buy the stock at $12.00 yet it is now only worth $5.00. This loss will be somewhat offset by the premium I received when I sold the option, but in reality this would only just cover the brokerage costs in such a transaction.

We will now look at the possible option positions and their implications.

Call Options

A call option provides the right but not the obligation to buy the underlying security at a fixed price on or before a set date. An NAB July 3500 call is the right but not the obligation to buy NAB at $35.00 on or before the expiry date in July. To obtain this right a premium is paid.

If a trader *buys* or *takes* a call option then this person's market view reflects the two following conditions:

1.   The underlying stock will increase in value.

2. The option is undervalued as a function of the option's pricing components and it will increase in value as a function of the increase in the value of one of these underlying components. (When traders talk about an option being undervalued they are generally referring to the option's current volatility when compared to its historic volatility. As will be discussed in depth later, when volatility increases so too do the prices of options.)

A call option buyer can lose no more than the premium paid to purchase the option.

The call option buyer may either exercise the option and take delivery of the underlying stock or choose to sell the option.

A trader who has bought a call option is said to be long the option and also long the underlying stock.

If a trader *sells* or *writes* a call option, this person's market view reflects the two following conditions:

1. That the underlying stock will either stay the same value or it will decrease in value.
2. That the option is overvalued and it will decrease in value due to a decrease in the option pricing components. As a consequence of this the option will expire worthless.

The call option writer is required to sell the underlying stock at a set price if called upon to do so.

The writer wants to avoid having the shares called away.

A naked option writer faces potentially unlimited loss and the potential profit is limited to the amount of premium received when the option was sold.

The option may expire worthless or the writer can buy the option back for a profit.

A trader who has written a call option is said to be short the option and also short the underlying stock.

Put Options

A put option gives the right but not the obligation to sell the underlying security at a set price on or before the expiry date. A WMC June 800 put is the right but not the obligation to sell WMC at $8.00 on or before the expiry date in June.

If a trader *buys* or *takes* a put option this person's market view reflects the following two market conditions:

1. The underlying stock will decline in value.
2. The option is undervalued as a function of the components of the option price. (Once again the component that traders generally talk about when assessing whether

an option is overpriced or underpriced is volatility. Volatility is non-directional, so an increase in volatility will affect both puts and calls. If volatility increases the value of the option will increase.)

A put option buyer can lose no more than the premium paid for the option.

The trader can either sell the put option or exercise it and sell the underlying shares.

A trader who has bought a put option is said to be long the put option but short the underlying stock.

If a trader *writes* or *sells* a put option, then this person's market view reflects the two following conditions:

1. The underlying stock will increase in value.

2. The option is considered to be overvalued.

A put option writer's profit is limited to the premium received in selling the option. A put option writer faces potentially unlimited risk. All put option writers are naked.

The option may expire worthless or the trader can buy it back at a profit.

A trader who has written a put option is said to be short the option but long the underlying stock.

The Components of an Options Contract

It will be apparent that options are standard contracts. The functioning of the options market is dependent upon this. It enables communication between options traders and a clear understanding of the rights and obligations specified in the contracts that are being traded.

The components of an options contract require closer examination.

Date of Expiry

Options move through a set calendar cycle that is fixed according to the underlying share. In addition to this quarterly cycle some stocks also have 'spot months'. These options are listed ten business days before the expiry of the nearest month. Some stocks have a rolling three-month spot expiry. These are all listed in the Appendix.

The Options Clearing House (OCH) stipulates that trading in options ceases at the close of trading on the Thursday preceding the last working Friday of the maturity month. If the Thursday falls on a public holiday, trading will cease on the last business day preceding the last Friday of the expiry month.

The OCH produces a calendar that lists each expiry date. This can be downloaded from: www.asx.com.au/markets/l4/OptionExpiryCalendar_AM4.shtm

Exercise Price (Strike Price)

This is the price at which an option buyer may exercise the right to buy or sell shares covered by a given options contract. Each exercise price is generally fixed throughout the life of the option, with exercise prices being set at the following intervals:

Stocks selling at:

    up to $1.00 at 10¢ intervals

    $1.00 to $4.99 at 25¢ intervals

    $5.00 to $9.99 at 50¢ intervals

    $10.00 and above at $1.00 intervals

Whilst these are generally fixed for the life of the option, they may be altered if the company whose shares are covered by the options makes a cash issue.

It is important to highlight the difference between the effects of cash issues and those of a bonus issue. A well-known practical example of this was the bid for Optus by SingTel. In the event of the bid being successful the following formula would be used to adjust the exercise or strike price for CWO:

New exercise price = (Old exercise price − $2.25) ÷ 0.8

As highlighted below a bonus issue results in both a change in strike price and the number of shares covered by the option. A cash issue does not alter the number of shares covered by an option contract since these shares do not accrue to the option contract unless the option is exercised on a cum-issue basis.

Number of Shares

An option contract generally gives the trader leverage over 1,000 shares of the underlying stock. However, this may change during the life of the option if the underlying stock is involved in a bonus issue. If for example a company declares a 1:1 bonus then there will be an additional 1,000 shares created with an exercise price half that of the original exercise price.

Premium

The quoted price of an option is more often known as the premium. Option prices are quoted on a per share basis, thus to obtain the full contract price a trader has to multiply the quoted price by 1,000. Hence, if BHP-Billiton July 1000 calls were trading at 10¢, the price of one contract would be 10¢ × 1,000 = $100.

An option premium splits naturally into two parts: intrinsic value and time value. Intrinsic value may be defined as the difference between the market value of an underlying security and the exercise price of a given option.

For example, if BHP-Billiton is trading at $10.10, then a BHP-Billiton July 1000 call option is said to have an intrinsic value of 10¢, this being the difference between the option strike price and the current price of the underlying stock. If this call is trading at 20¢, 10¢ of this is the intrinsic value. The remaining 10¢ represents the time value left in the option. If our option price had remained the same whilst BHP-Billiton was trading at $10.15 then our intrinsic value would have been 15¢ and our time value would 5¢.

The formula for determining the intrinsic value of a call option is as follows:

Call intrinsic value* = Current share price – Strike price

* This number can never be less than 0

The formula for determining a put option's intrinsic value is as follows:

Put intrinsic value* = Strike price – Current share price

* This number can never be less than 0

As an option moves towards expiry the amount of time value contained within the premium will decrease at an accelerating rate until an option has no time value left. In such situations an option will only trade at its intrinsic value.

A further refinement to our description can be added by the introduction of the terms in-the-money (ITM), at-the-money (ATM) and out-of-the-money (OTM).

A call option is said to be in-the-money if the stock price is above the strike price of the option, and it is out-of-the-money if the stock price is below the option strike price. If a call option is out-of-the-money, it naturally has no intrinsic value and its premium merely represents its time value.

Put options work in reverse. A put option is said to be in-the-money if the stock price is below the option strike price and out-of-the-money if the stock price is above the strike price.

Both put and call options have their greatest amount of time value when the stock price is equal to the exercise price. In such a situation an option is said to be at-the-money. As an option becomes either deeply in-the-money or out-of-the-money, its time value will shrink rapidly. This tends to be more evident in put options, which decrease in time value at a greater rate once they go in-the-money compared to an equivalent call option. As we will see later, this feature is of some importance. At-the-money options are composed of only time value. Only in-the-money options have any intrinsic value at expiry.

The relationship between share price, strike price and the concepts of in-the-money, at-the-money and out-of-the-money can be seen in the following table.

Table 1.1 *Price Relationship*

Underlying Share Price $28.00		
Strike	**Call**	**Put**
2650	ITM	OTM
2700	ITM	OTM
2750	ITM	OTM
2800	ATM	ATM
2850	OTM	ITM
2900	OTM	ITM

Reading Option Quotes

The reading of option quotes is only slightly different from reading equity quotes. Call option quote tables are given in all major daily newspapers and the *Australian Financial Review*. A fictitious example is shown below.

Table 1.2 *Option Quote Table*

Up to 4.56pm February 9, 2002				XYZ Last sale price $11.81		
Stock	Strike Price	Buyer	Seller	Last Sale	T.O. '000	Open Int.
2002						
Mar	9.30	2.46	2.64	2.93		25
Mar	9.79	2.05	2.15	1.56		253
Mar	10.28	1.50	1.66	1.54		726
Mar	10.77	1.03	1.17	1.05		101
Mar	11.26	.59	.71	.59	15	536
Mar	11.75	.31	.37	.36	60	874

These tables are largely self-explanatory, however there are a few important features that traders need to be aware of.

When reading from left to right the option exercise month and then the strike price are shown. There are then two columns showing the current buyer and seller quotes. It is here that traders will need to be a little careful. If we examine the first quote series the XYZ March 930 call is bid $2.46, offered $2.64, yet the last sale was $2.93. This last sale is referred to as being stale in that it was obviously some time ago, and is not reflective of current price action. There is a simple way to see whether a last sale is stale and that is to look in the column marked T.O. (turnover). This column is the number of option contracts traded that day—if there is no number in this column then the last sale price is irrelevant.

The next column is called Open Int., or Open Interest to give it its full name. Open interest refers to the number of option contracts currently open for that particular series. From the earlier section you will remember that options are a contract, they have two parties. When those two parties come together open interest goes up by one contract. As we will see later open interest is an important feature when deciding which option to trade.

At this point I need to introduce another warning. If you are relying on yesterday's paper for your information you are doomed to failure. The trading of options requires access to real-time information. As we will see later, this real-time information will also need to include a great deal more than simply price.

Building Blocks

In later chapters I will look at a variety of options strategies. However, what I need to point out is that all options strategies are made up of only six building blocks, and if you can understand these building blocks then understanding the more complex strategies will be that much easier.

The six basic building blocks are:

1. Buy the underlying stock.
2. Short sell the underlying stock.
3. Buy a call (long call).
4. Sell a call (short call).
5. Buy a put (long put).
6. Sell a put (short put).

1. Buy the Underlying Stock

Buying the underlying stock is an extremely basic step that all who contemplate options trading should be intimately familiar with. Our risk is limited to the amount that we paid for the share and the potential reward is theoretically unlimited. Being long the underlying is a bullish strategy—it is only undertaken when you believe the stock price will advance.

Figure 1.1 represents a long stock position. This payoff diagram represents the purchase of a share at $12.50. The breakeven price is the point at which the x-axis is penetrated. (In these examples costs have been excluded.)

In undertaking this position we can lose no more than the $12.50 (per share) the share was purchased for, so the risk is limited. The potential reward is theoretically unlimited as shares have an unbounded upside.

Figure 1.1 Long Stock Payoff Diagram

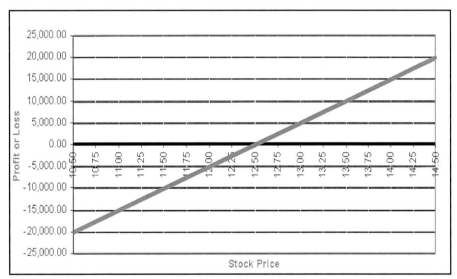

2. Short Sell the Underlying Stock

Contrary to popular opinion short selling is not illegal in Australia. Short selling is permitted on some 250-plus ASX listed shares. Short selling is the technique by which you short sell a stock which you do not own in the belief that you can buy the share back at a lower price, thereby closing out the trade at a profit. You of course have to 'borrow' the shares to do this. When you short sell a share you are bearish that particular share.

Short selling is subject to certain rules, such as the type of share that can be short sold. Not every share can be short sold. A complete list of those that can is available from the ASX. Traders must also be aware of the uptick rule. This prevents very large traders from simply short selling large quantities of stock into the market and driving the price down. Short sales are also subject to a margin, which is generally in the order of 20%, so if I short sold $100,000 worth of shares I would have to lodge a $20,000 margin with my broker. This margin is marked to market every day, so if the value of the stock that was short sold climbed to $110,000 I would have to lodge an additional $2,000 to maintain the margin at 20%.

It is important to be aware in short selling that you face a theoretically unlimited risk on the upside, and you will be responsible for any dividends that are paid by the company during the period the short sale is open.

Figure 1.2 represents the payoff diagram for a short sold stock position.

Figure 1.2 *Short Sold Stock Payoff Diagram*

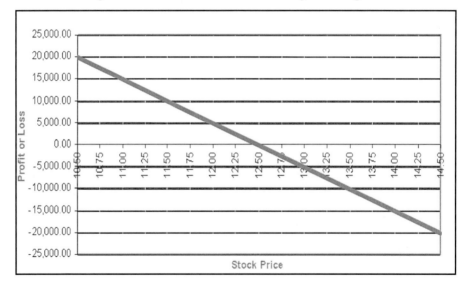

3. Long Call

Being long a call is a bullish strategy. The owner of a call has the same theoretical profit potential as the holder of the underlying share but with much lower risk. The lower risk is simply brought about by the leverage provided by outlaying a lesser amount of capital.

Figure 1.3 represents a long call payoff position. The grey, curved line in this figure (and all subsequent payoff diagrams) represents the result if the position is closed 21 days from expiry. The black, straight line represents the result if the position is closed at expiry.

Figure 1.3 *Long Call Payoff Diagram*

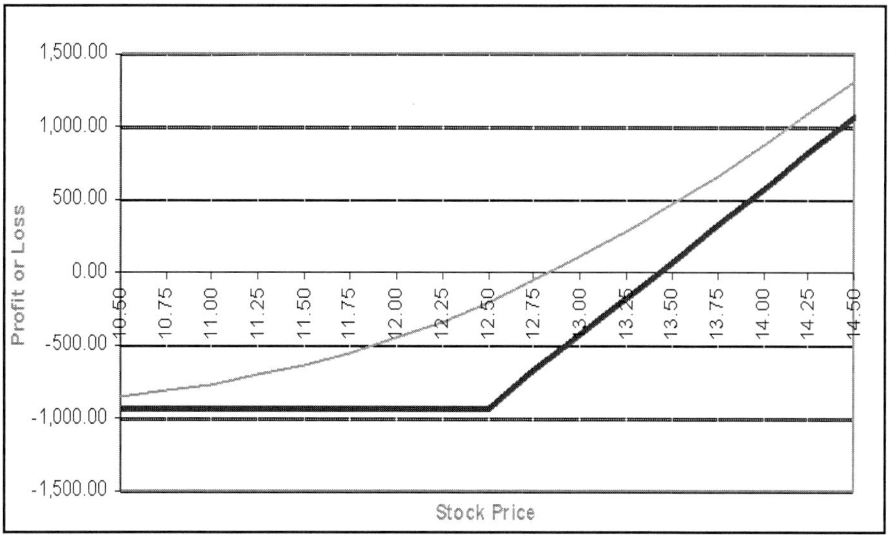

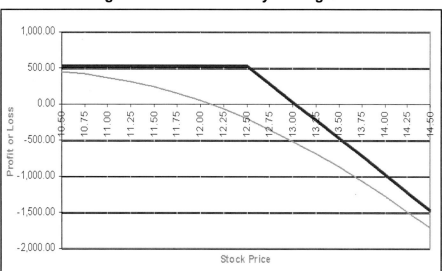

4. Short Call

Selling a call is a bearish strategy and exposes the writer to a potentially unlimited loss and limited profit. The profit is limited to the premium received for the option. Short calls will incur cash margins (discussed later) unless they are covered by scrip. Short calls that are covered by scrip are referred to as covered calls. Being short a call has the payoff diagram below.

Figure 1.4 *Short Call Payoff Diagram*

5. Long Put

Being long a put is a bearish strategy. The potential payoff is equivalent to a short stock position but the risk with a long put is limited to the amount of premium paid for the put. The long put payoff diagram is shown in Figure 1.5.

Figure 1.5   *Long Put Payoff Diagram*

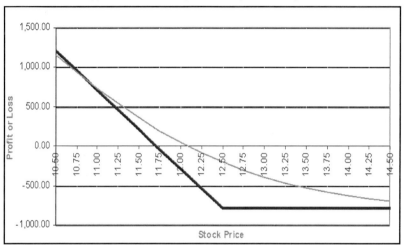

6. Short Put

A short put is a bullish position. It has potentially unlimited risk and limited profit. The loss characteristic is equivalent to a long stock position but with far less potential for upside than a long stock position. Figure 1.6 illustrates the payoff diagram for a short put.

Figure 1.6   *Short Put Payoff Diagram*

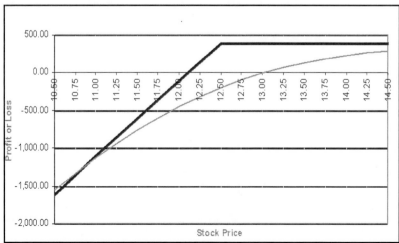

Margins

It will be remembered from our earlier discussions that a written call may be either covered or naked. A covered call is one that is written directly against an underlying share that you already own. If you do not own the underlying share and you have written a call then it is said to be naked. (By definition all written puts are effectively naked; it is of no consequence whether you own the underlying share and write the put since ownership of the underlying share confers no 'protection' to the written position.)

When a naked written call or put position is initiated, margins are payable to your broker, who in turn lodges them with the Options Clearing House (OCH). The OCH calculates margins using a system known as TIMS (Theoretical Intermarket Margining System). TIMS takes into account the volatility of the underlying security when calculating margin obligations.

The total margin is made up of two components:

1. The *premium margin* is the market value of the particular position (the value of the call, not the value of the share) at the close of business each day. It represents the amount that would be required to close out your option position.

2. The *risk margin* covers the potential change in the price of the option contract assuming the maximum probable inter-day movement (daily volatility) in the price of the underlying security. The daily volatility figure, expressed as a percentage, is known as the *margin interval.*

For example let's assume that we have written a BHP-Billiton 1000 call for 45¢, the current price of BHP-Billiton is $9.80 and the current margin interval for BHP-Billiton is 10%. The amount we have written the call for is defined as the premium margin and this will alter each day as the closing price of the written call varies. For example, if the call fell to 38¢ the premium margin would be adjusted downwards; if the call rose to 55¢ the premium margin would be adjusted upwards. A simple way to remember the value of the premium margin is to simply look at the liquidation value of the option.

The premium margin is only the first part of the margining calculation. The second part is the risk margin. The key to the risk margin is the margin interval. In a worst-case scenario (in this example) it is possible for BHP-Billiton to move either +10% or –10% of its current value (10% of $9.80, which is 98¢). It is therefore deemed possible for BHP-Billiton to move either up to $10.78 or down to $8.82.

What the risk margin calculation does is give a theoretical price to our written option based upon the assumption that BHP-Billiton was trading at the higher value determined by the margin interval. So assume that this higher value gave our option a theoretical value of 75¢. The risk margin would be the worst-case scenario of 75¢. The current market close of the option is 45¢ so the risk margin payable is 30¢.

The total margin payable is the premium margin of 45¢, plus the risk margin of 30¢, which is equal to 75¢. The total amount we would have to lodge with the OCH for this position is $750 per contract (1,000 shares at 75¢ margin each).

The situation for written puts is exactly the same in that the premium margin is the marked to market value of the written put and the risk margin is calculated by assuming a worst-case scenario move on the downside.

If these figures seem rather complicated, don't despair—an online facility provided by the ASX will calculate the appropriate margin levels for you before a strategy is entered into. The margin estimator is available at: www10.asx.com.au/asx/OpcStart?Mode=M

The ASX will accept a variety of instruments as collateral for option writing. It is possible to lodge cash, shares, bank guarantees and certain securities such as certificates of deposit. Typically if you lodge shares the ASX will assign a marginable value to them. What this means is that the full value will not be marginable but rather a proportion of the full value. The amount the shares are reduced by is termed a 'haircut' and is typically 30%.

A full list of eligible collateral is available from:

www.asx.com.au/markets/l4/EligibleCollateral_AM4.shtm

Margins are discussed further in Chapter 5.

Many option trades also allow for what are known as 'offsets'. An offset occurs when one option protects another. For example, if I have taken out a bull spread by buying a 1000 call and selling a 1050 call I have an offset since my obligation incurred by writing the 1050 call is protected by owning the 1000 call. These are discussed further in Chapter 5.

This chapter is an extract from Christopher Tate's Option Trader Home Study Course.

(See the back of this book for more information.)

2

Option Pricing

By the end of this chapter you should be able to:

▶ Describe the two major option pricing models.

▶ Distinguish between the option pricing models.

▶ Describe the advantages and disadvantages of each of the option pricing models.

▶ Understand the major factors influencing the price of an option.

▶ Understand volatility and its role in option pricing.

▶ Use technology to assist in the pricing of options.

Pricing an Option

Initially option pricing seems to be a very daunting subject. There are some mathematical concepts to come to terms with and some statistical measures to understand. Unfortunately for those of you who lack confidence in these areas it is impossible to adequately describe options pricing without a journey into mathematics. Fortunately all the necessary calculations can be performed by readily available software, though the concepts still need to be mastered.

The question may be asked as to why it is necessary to understand options pricing. Doesn't the market determine the price you can either buy or sell an option for? This is partly true. The market does to a degree dictate our actions as traders; but think of options valuation in the way you would think of valuing a business. If an option is believed to be undervalued compared to its historical norm then you would prefer to be an option buyer. However, if an option were considered overvalued, it would be wise to be an option seller. The only way a judgement can be made as to whether an option is over or undervalued is to be able to price the option accurately.

Option Pricing Background

Before 1973 the answer to the question 'How much is an option worth?' required very tedious and laborious mathematical equations. The equations took so long to solve that by the time any meaningful answer had been arrived at the potential trade that was under consideration had long since passed. This lack of a workable model was a major handicap for options traders and led to some catastrophic losses as traders effectively tried to 'wing it' and guess at the appropriate value for an option.

The Black-Scholes Pricing Model

In 1973 the problem of a robust options pricing methodology was largely solved by the work of Fischer Black and Myron Scholes. This model—which became known as the Black-Scholes model, for which its authors received a Nobel Prize—had a limited number of inputs and could be programmed into the newly emerging pocket calculators. This meant that traders could quickly and accurately generate prices for options.

The Black-Scholes model is represented by the following equation:

$$c = SN(d_1) - Xe^{-rT}N(d_2)$$

$$p = Xe^{-rT}N(-d_2) - SN(-d_1)$$

$$d_1 = \frac{\ln(S/X) + (r + \sigma^2/2)T}{\sigma\sqrt{T}}$$

$$d_2 = d_1 - \sigma\sqrt{T}$$

S = Stock price

X = Strike price of option

r = Risk-free interest rate

T   =   Time to expiration in years

σ =   Volatility of the relative price change of the underlying stock price

N(x) =   The cumulative normal distribution function

ln   =   The natural logarithm

In this equation the inputs are limited to:

1.   The price of the underlying stock.

2.   The strike price of the option.

3.   The current risk-free rate of return.

4.   The time left to expiry.

5.   The volatility of the underlying stock.

The original model proposed by Black and Scholes did have some deficiencies in that it assumed all options were European in nature and therefore no early exercise was permitted. Nor did it take into consideration dividend payments. After its introduction Black and Scholes realised that the majority of stocks do pay dividends and that ETOs—with a limited number of exceptions—are American in nature in that they allow early exercise. Hence a modification to the formula was necessary to take into account these factors.

Most online calculators still use a variation of the Black-Scholes model simply because of the speed of calculation it provides. However, to do any detailed investigation into early exercise, the so-called binomial model must be used.

The Binomial Pricing Model

The binomial model is sometimes referred to by its full name, the Cox, Ross and Rubenstein model. This model has the same inputs as the Black-Scholes model with an additional input for the dividend payment. This model makes the assumption that over time the underlying share can move either up or down by a given amount. Using this information the model builds a tree of possible values for the option at various points in time. The end result is a branching structure that looks like Figure 2.1 (overleaf).

This branching structure effectively looks back in time and gives a series of values for a given option at those times based upon the volatility of the underlying share.

The advantage of the binomial model is its ability to take into account the possibility that an option may be subject to early exercise. Its major disadvantage is that it is computationally intensive and it is therefore difficult to use to price chains of options.

Figure 2.1 *Binomial Tree*

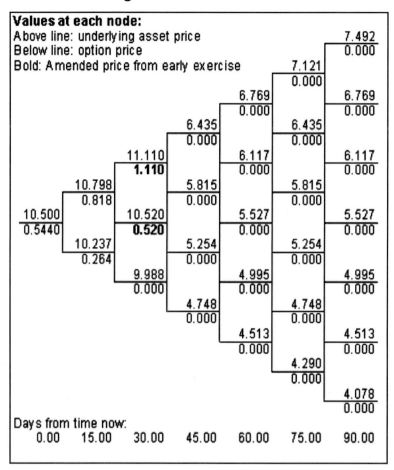

Values at each node:
Above line: underlying asset price
Below line: option price
Bold: Amended price from early exercise

Days from time now:

| 0.00 | 15.00 | 30.00 | 45.00 | 60.00 | 75.00 | 90.00 |

Factors Influencing Option Pricing

1. Stock Price

It should be apparent that the price of the underlying stock is extremely important in the pricing of an option. Any change in the price of the underlying will be immediately reflected in the price of the option. As the price of the underlying rises so too will the price of call options. As the price of the underlying falls the price of call options will fall, whereas the price of put options will rise.

It may seem obvious that you would want to be long calls and short puts when a stock is trending up or the reverse when it is trending down. But identifying and staying with the trend is extremely difficult for traders. For example, consider the following chart of NAB during a sequence of upward moves.

Figure 2.2 *NAB with Volume and MACD Histogram*

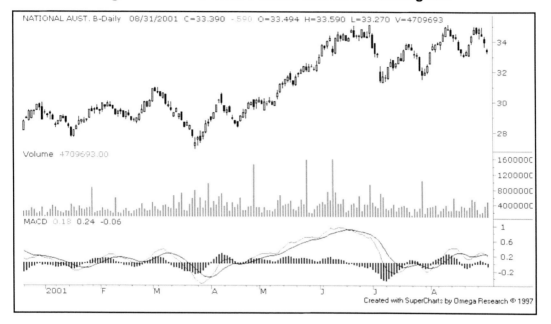

This is a basic candlestick chart with a MACD crossover system. The vertical bars in the middle level of the chart represent volume. Examine the move up in share price from April to June. During this period NAB moved from $27.00 to $35.00, and throughout this period there were market participants who were selling NAB (note the volume levels) despite the evidence that the stock was moving higher. The first and only rule of trend trading is that you follow the trend until you think it is going to end. An inability to follow the trend is a simple case of lost opportunity. In the tech wreck of 2000 an inability to trade according to the trend would have been disastrous since many domestic technology stocks lost almost 98% of their value.

In trading, the trend rules. Ignore it at your own peril.

2. Exercise Price

The strike or exercise price in options pricing is intimately linked to the impact of the price of the underlying share. It will be remembered from Chapter 1 that an option's premium is made up of two components; intrinsic value and time value. Intrinsic value represents what the position would be worth if it were exercised immediately, however this value can only go to zero. Time value represents the sum total of what the market believes about the future value of the underlying share. Only options that are in-the-money have any intrinsic value. Options that are at-the-money or out-of-the-money have only time value.

As the exercise price increases the value of calls *decreases* whereas the value of puts *increases*. Conversely, as the exercise price decreases the value of call options *increases* whereas the value of put options *decreases*.

3. Interest Rates (Risk-Free Rates)

Whereas the previous two inputs into an options pricing model allowed no room for interpretation, the appropriate level of interest rate for inclusion into the equation can be a matter of debate. Short-term options may require the input of the current 90-day bank bill rate whereas a longer-term option or a warrant may require a longer-dated security such as the three-year bond rate. A list of current rates can be obtained from the Reserve Bank of Australia at: www.rba.gov.au.

To understand the impact of interest rates upon options it is necessary to understand the concept of carrying costs. To illustrate this, consider the situation of a trader who had established a long options position—an option buyer. In such a situation it is assumed that the trader has to pay interest on the funds used to purchase the options. Whilst this assumption is generally not true it is used because if the trader had not purchased the options then these funds could have remained on deposit and have been earning interest. Hence, there is an opportunity cost involved in buying options that needs to be balanced against the possible return from the bought positions.

A trader who has taken up a written position in options receives interest from the funds on deposit. Because the trading of options and associated stock will result in either a credit or debit balance being generated the cost of interest rates needs to be factored into the options pricing equation.

As short-term interest rates rise the value of call options *increases* whereas the value of put options *decreases*. Conversely if short-term interest rates fall the value of call options *decreases* and the value of put options *increases*.

An example of the impact of changes in interest rates can be seen in Figure 2.3 (opposite).

There is also a relationship between interest rates and time; the longer the life of an option the greater the impact of changes in interest rates upon the option's future value. This relationship will be explored more fully in the next chapter when we examine option sensitivities, or the 'Greeks' as they are more commonly known

Figure 2.3 *Impact of Interest Rate Changes*

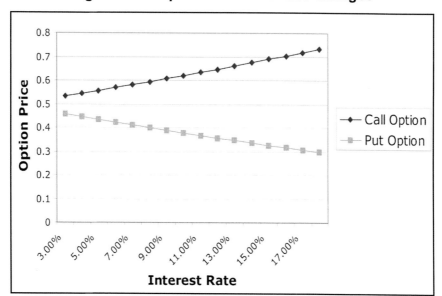

Having reviewed the impact of interest rates upon option prices, I should mention that this is a comparatively minor issue due to the relative stability of interest rates over the life of the majority of options.

4. Time to Expiry

Options are a wasting asset that are subject to the use 'em or lose 'em maxim. The greater the time to expiration the greater the value of the option. Time essentially equals opportunity; the greater the time value of the option the greater the potential for the option to expire in-the-money. As such, traders are willing to pay more for longer-dated options since this translates into buying opportunity. Remember this is only potential; trading in long-dated options does not automatically guarantee success.

The rate of time decay for in-the-money, at-the-money and out-of-the-money options is not the same. The rate of time decay for out-of-the-money and in-the-money options is greater than that for at-the-money options due to the fact that they have lower time values.

An increase in the time until expiry will *increase* both call and put prices, whereas a decrease in the time till expiry will *decrease* both call and put prices. Examples of the influence of time are shown in Figures 2.4 and 2.5, overleaf.

Figure 2.4   *Option Time Decay*

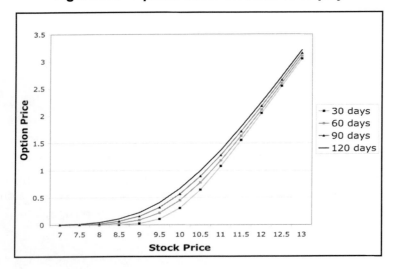

Figure 2.5   *Option Value vs Time to Expiry*

5. Dividends

A dividend is simply a cash disbursement to shareholders. As the dividend rate increases the value of calls *decreases* and the value of puts *increases*. Conversely, as the payout rate decreases the value of calls *increases* and the value of puts *decreases*.

The simple answer as to why this occurs may simply be that when a share goes ex-dividend then the share price adjusts by the amount of the dividend. Hence call options will decrease in value and put options will increase in value. However, this explanation is too simple and does not take into account the fact that option traders know several months in advance when a dividend will be struck and they adjust option prices accordingly.

A common misconception among people who are new to options trading is that it is possible, for example, to buy a put option the day before a stock goes ex-dividend and then profit from the stock's adjustment when it goes ex-dividend. This is a naive assumption since the option price already has the dividend factored in.

To understand fully why dividends impact on option prices in the way that they do it is necessary to review the costs associated with owning a share. Traders who own a given stock will receive dividends. They will also incur any costs—such as the cost of borrowing— associated with owning the share. This is considered not to be an issue since the dividend offsets these costs. Hence, owning the underlying share is considered to be desirable. However, owning the equivalent call option is not desirable in this way since the benefit of the dividend stream does not accrue to the holder of the call.

Puts, however, will increase in value when a dividend is struck because the alternative to owning a put is to short sell the underlying share. The short seller is responsible for the payment of the dividend. This feature makes short selling a stock that is going ex-dividend unattractive. Conversely it makes owning the equivalent put option position attractive to traders. An example of the effects of dividends is shown below.

Figure 2.6 *Impact of Dividends*

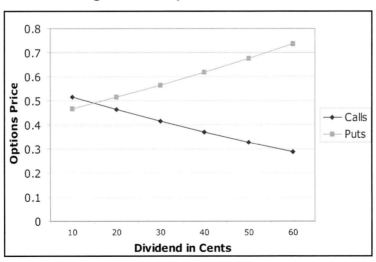

A full list of dividend payment dates is available in PDF format from:

www.egoli.com.au/egoli_frame.asp?Frame=Research

www.asx.com.au/markets/l4/Notices_AM4.shtm

The ASX option pricing calculator will also automatically build dividend payments into the pricing equation. This makes the task of finding accurate information much easier.

The fact that companies pay a dividend introduces an additional layer of complexity to some option trades. You will remember from Chapter 1 that ETOs are American in character; they can be exercised at any time. As such it may be viable for a trader to exercise the option early in order to capture the dividend.

To illustrate this, consider the following example.

NAB is trading at $30.00, the near month 2900 call is trading at $1.00 and the stock has a 30¢ dividend about to be paid.

In this situation a call option buyer has three alternatives. Firstly, the trader could continue to hold the option; secondly the trader could exercise the call option; or thirdly sell the call option and buy the underlying stock.

Holding onto the option will incur a loss of 30¢ because both the stock and the option will adjust for the dividend. Exercising the option will result in a purchase of the stock at $29.00; the $1.00 from the option is foregone since it has been exercised. The true purchase price for the stock is therefore $30.00 (exercise price of $29.00 plus $1.00 profit foregone from the option). The stock adjusts by 30¢ but this loss is offset by the dividend of 30¢. This results in a breakeven trade, which is superior to simply holding the call option, since such a strategy resulted in a loss of 30¢.

The final alternative is to sell the option at market and buy the underlying stock on the market. If the option is trading at the same price the trader paid for it ($1.00 in this case), then this strategy would have the same result as simply exercising the option. However, if the option is trading at $1.50 as opposed to $1.00 (for this example), then this strategy would be the same as simply exercising the option, but the sale of the option would yield a 50¢ profit per contract.

Dividends and Early Exercise

The aim of understanding early exercise is twofold. Firstly, by not understanding the alternatives open to them option holders may not be maximising their potential profit. If an option is either exercised too early or held too long the trade may not turn out to be as profitable as it could be. Secondly a call option writer must be aware of the possibility of taking evasive action to avoid having the stock called away at an inopportune time. This is important because if an option is exercised the day before the ex-dividend date, the writer receives the exercise notice on the ex-dividend date. The writer therefore has to deliver the stock with the dividend, thereby possibly incurring a substantial loss.

The early exercise of put options is a slightly different situation. The early exercise of a put option is really only viable when the option is deep in-the-money and the remaining time value is effectively zero. The early exercise of a put option needs to balance the loss of the dividend against the interest that could be generated by placing the funds on deposit. More often than not, puts are exercised on the ex-dividend date.

Fortunately for traders there is some very clever software that has been developed to assist in determining the potential for early exercise. The following diagram is from Peter Hoadley, who has developed a variety of option-related software. This software is available from:

www.hoadley.net/Options/options.htm

Figure 2.7 *Early Exercise Calculation*

Theoretical Early Exercise Thresholds for American Options

| Binomial Tree Steps: | 30 |
| Number of decimal places for put prices: | 3 |

Trade	Type	Strike	Underlying Asset Price	Optimal Early Exercise Threshold	Option Price at	Find Early Exercise Points
						Note:
Option Trade 1	Call	33.00		Early exercise not optimal		Press the above button to search current strategy (as displayed on the strategy
Option Trade 2	Put	33.00	28.500	On or after 07/07/2002	0.0000	evaluation sheet) for optimal early exercise
			29.000	On or after 07/07/2002	0.0000	points.
			29.500	On or after 07/21/2002	0.0000	
			30.000	On or after 08/19/2002	0.0000	The underlying asset prices
			30.500	On or after 09/06/2002	0.0000	considered are those on the
			31.000	On or after 09/16/2002	0.0000	pay-off diagram on the strategy
			31.500	On or after 09/23/2002	0.0000	evaluation sheet. To evaluate a
			32.000	On or after 09/26/2002	0.0000	different range of prices, change
						the 'price in the centre of the graph'
Option Trade 3	Put	32.00	28.500	On or after 07/12/2002	0.0000	and the 'graph increment' settings.
			29.000	On or after 08/15/2002	0.0000	
			29.500	On or after 09/04/2002	0.0000	The early exercise threshold is
			30.000	On or after 09/15/2002	0.0000	the theoretical optimal time for
			30.500	On or after 09/22/2002	0.0000	early exercise. In practice, bid/ask
			31.000	On or after 09/26/2002	0.0000	spreads, brokerage, and other market
						conditions can change this
						threshold significantly.
						More Information:
						http://www.hoadley.net/Options/FAQs.htm#Early Exercise

Reproduced with the permission of Peter Hoadley.

I need to introduce a note of caution regarding early exercise calculations. The calculations for early exercise are—like many financial calculations—based upon the assumption that the market and its participants behave in a rational manner. Anyone who has been in the market for any period of time can tell you that neither the market nor its participants are rational. In the options market people do stupid things all the time, and that includes exercising options they should not in their right minds have exercised. So if you are an options writer, be diligent in understanding the possibility of early exercise, but always keep in mind how illogical and poorly advised other traders can be.

6. Volatility

I have saved the most important component of options pricing until last.

All option trading revolves around an understanding of volatility.

In presenting this section on volatility it will be necessary for me to explore a few probability concepts. I urge you to try to understand the concepts and not just the computations that drive them. Where possible I will direct you to freely available tools that will do all the number crunching for you. However I must warn you, if you do not understand the concepts then it will be impossible for you to understand the outputs of the tools I will refer you to. If you struggle with this section you may email me for clarification and assistance (info@artoftrading.com.au).

Before we begin it is necessary for me to point out a few basic points concerning volatility:

- A failure to understand volatility will lead to a failure to be able to trade options.

- Volatility is simply a measure of the speed and magnitude of stock price movement.

- Volatility is not directly observable. The other factors influencing an option's price can be directly observed.

- Volatility has no bias; there is no such thing as upward or downward volatility, so when you see a talking head on television talking about upside volatility you can be assured that this person is a fool and worthy of your scorn.

- The greater the volatility, the greater the probability that a stock will either do well or do poorly.

Before looking in depth at volatility, it is important to understand that trend and volatility are not the same. Volatility is the tendency for prices to fluctuate. For example, consider the chart of NCP on the following page.

It is obvious that during the period under study the prevailing trend is down. This is a description of the direction of price action, it is not a description of the volatility of the distribution of price. If I were to describe the volatility of price I would need to know something about the distribution of prices from one period to the next. This period may be daily, weekly or monthly.

What I propose to do is to take you through a series of steps to explain the importance of volatility. We have already seen that volatility and trend are not the same thing. It is now necessary to start to understand volatility.

Figure 2.8 *NCP Daily Chart*

Step 1 – Distribution

The first step towards understanding volatility is to understand the concepts upon which much of probability theory is based. It is therefore necessary to understand how prices are distributed from one trading period to the next and to get a feeling for the likelihood of any given price movement.

Most of the statistics of probability are built upon the assumption that the trials being conducted are random in nature. The same applies to the assumptions that are made about the statistical nature of trading. It is assumed that markets are random and that one event does not necessarily influence the next. (There is actually a great deal of debate as to whether markets are random, and a discussion of this is beyond the scope of this text. However, for the sake of argument consider the two charts on the following page. Can you pick which of these was generated randomly? The answer is at the end of the chapter.)

In studying the probabilities of markets we want to know the chance of the share price moving a given amount either up or down in a given period. To get an understanding of how likely movements are we need to know how price is distributed. We need to somehow work out how price moves from one time to the next.

Figure 2.9

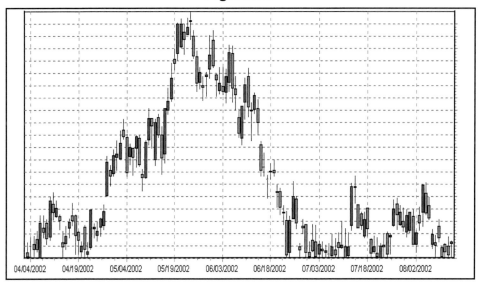

Figure 2.10

To describe an event that is random we need to look at a distribution curve. A distribution curve is simply a picture that gives us an idea of the outcome of events. To illustrate how this works, consider the following example. Imagine there is an orange tree with the fruit dropping off it. Each orange drops on the ground and ends up a certain distance from the trunk of the tree, on either side. Some oranges stay where they fall and are close to the trunk, some roll along the ground after they fall and are therefore further away. If we map where each orange lands, we would end up with a chart that looks like Figure 2.11 (or Figure 2.12 when plotted as a line).

Figure 2.11 *Normal Distribution of Results*

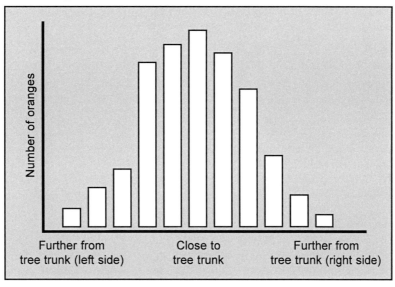

Figure 2.12 *Normal Distribution Plotted as a Line*

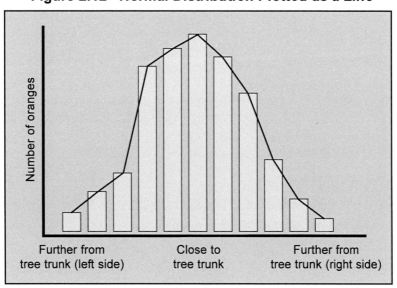

These are so-called frequency distributions. The curve they form is known as a normal distribution curve (or a bell curve). As you would expect the majority of oranges will land close to the tree trunk with fewer and fewer oranges landing further away.

The immediate question is: how does understanding distribution help us in trading? Consider this scenario: imagine you are an option trader and you are bullish about NCP. There are a range of options you could purchase but you want to know the probability of a given move in NCP. Knowing the underlying trend doesn't really help you because that does not convey the speed or magnitude of price movements. The only way the question as to which option to purchase can be answered is by understanding the distribution of NCP prices. Is the stock going to be sufficiently volatile over the period you are interested in trading to move prices enough to make the trade profitable?

To answer the question as to whether prices are volatile enough, it is necessary to understand what various volatility distributions look like. Some examples are shown in the figures opposite.

The shapes of these curves initially cause problems for traders who are new to them. The natural assumption is that the higher the peaks in the curve the higher the volatility. But remember we are interested in the speed and magnitude of movement, so the curves that flatten out represent very volatile movements (the results are more spread out), whereas those that are tall and skinny represent less volatile movements (the results are grouped together).

Step 2 – Describing the Curve

Normal distributions are referred to as being bell shaped and they can be described using two statistical tools; the mean and standard deviation.

If the curve is described as a normal distribution then we can assume that it is symmetrical about the mean. The mean corresponds to the peak of the curve, so we simply locate the value that corresponds with the peak. The mean can also be easily calculated. For example, if we took a week of share price data and calculated the mean price we could get the following:

$$(\$16.67 + \$16.54 + \$16.57 + \$16.85 + \$17.07) \div 5 = \$16.74$$

The average price for this week's worth of data is $16.74. Notice that most of the prices are clustered close to this figure. This is what we would expect and what our experience of share prices tells us. The majority of prices seem to centre around a mean value, and occasionally we get a large move away from that mean value.

Figure 2.13 *Low Volatility Distribution*

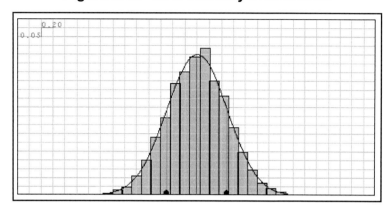

Figure 2.14 *Moderate Volatility Distribution*

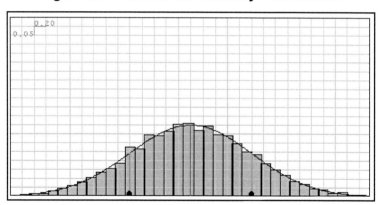

Figure 2.15 *High Volatility Distribution*

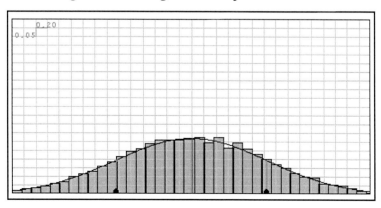

If we refer back to the earlier examples of normal distributions with differing volatilities it can be seen that the centre of the peak is the mean and prices disperse themselves around that peak. The distribution with the highest volatility spreads out fastest whereas in the low volatility curve the majority of values cluster close to the mean.

The statistic known as standard deviation gives us an idea of how often we can expect prices to cluster near the mean, and equally importantly how often we can expect prices to deviate by large amounts from the mean. So the standard deviation tells us how quickly prices spread out from the mean.

By definition:

1. 68.3% of all outcomes will fall between +1 and –1 standard deviation from the mean (about 2/3).

2. 95.4% of all outcomes will fall between +2 and –2 standard deviations from the mean (about 19/20).

3. 99.7% of all outcomes will fall between +3 and –3 standard deviations from the mean (about 369/370).

For example, if it were assumed that fictitious share XYZ were described by a normal distribution and I took a year's worth of trading history and analysed it, I might find the following:

Mean	18.48
Standard error	0.16
Median	17.85
Mode	18.04
Standard deviation	2.62

The average price for XYZ during the sample period was $18.48 and the standard deviation was $2.62. If I were to look at the XYZ chart I would see that on 172 of the 254 days analysed XYZ had a price that fell between $15.86 and $21.10. On 242 days I would see that it had a price that fell between $13.24 and $23.72. On 253 of the days analysed the price fell somewhere between $10.62 and $26.34. This is shown in Figure 2.16, opposite.

The data that has been analysed so far was for 254 trading days. Option traders deal in timeframes that are much shorter than this, so whilst analysing data for this length of time has helped illustrate some of the key concepts of describing normal curves it is of little practical use in options trading. To make this form of analysis appropriate for options trading, the timeframe needs to be shortened.

Figure 2.16 *Frequency Distribution for XYZ*

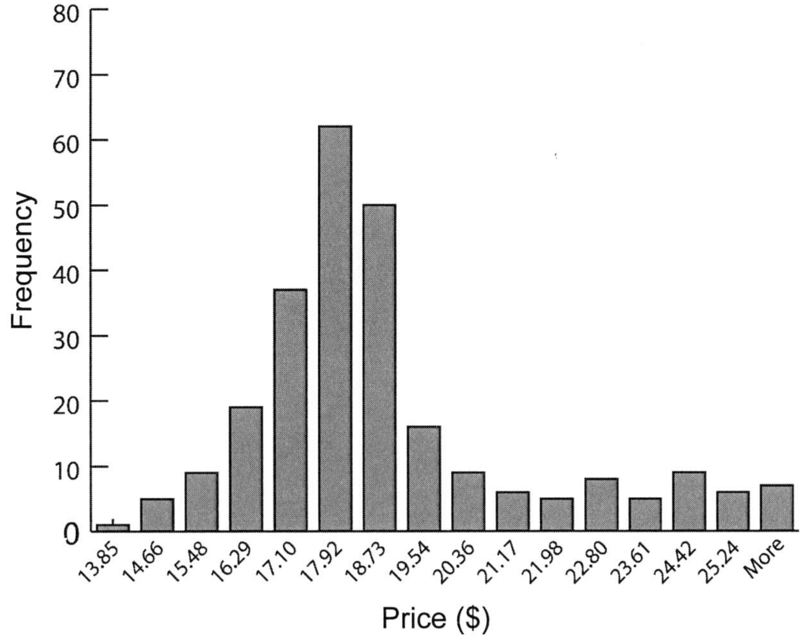

For example, consider the following trading scenario. Assume we are trading XYZ and it is currently sitting on its mean for the past 30 days of $17.61, and that we are looking to buy 1900 calls that expire in 30 days. This is quite a narrow timeframe for a call purchase so our analysis needs to be precise. We need to know what the likelihood is of XYZ hitting $19.00 or better within 30 days.

The data below reflects the 30 days trading in XYZ.

Mean	17.61
Standard Error	0.15
Median	17.83
Mode	18.20
Standard Deviation	0.72

This data tells us that the current standard deviation for XYZ is 72¢. To be profitable we need XYZ to be above $19.00 in 30 days. The question is, what is the probability of such an event occurring? A rough probability can be generated quite easily.

Effectively this trade requires XYZ to be approximately 2 standard deviations from the mean in 30 days time. The earlier discussion showed that the probability of a move beyond 2 standard deviations is approximately 1 in 20. Such odds are not very good.

Step 3 – Quantifying Volatility

The volatility used in option pricing is expressed as a percentage over a given timeframe. So if volatility is expressed as a percentage and standard deviation is a raw number, the question is, how do we get from the percentage to a raw dollar amount?

The answer is actually fairly simple. The volatility percentage of any given stock actually represents 1 standard deviation for a 1-year period. For example, if a $5.00 stock has a volatility of 25%, a price change of 1 standard deviation is $1.25 (25% of $5.00). Therefore in 1 year of trading it is probable that on 2 out of every 3 occasions the stock will trade somewhere between $3.75 and $6.25; that is +1 or –1 standard deviation. On 19 out of 20 occasions it will be trading between $2.50 and $7.50; that is +2 or –2 standard deviations. And on 369 out of 370 cases it will be trading somewhere between $1.25 and $8.75; that is +3 or –3 standard deviations.

Note however that this is a yearly figure. Option trading involves timeframes that are much shorter than this, therefore some adjustments need to be made to arrive at a relevant figure.

Again achieving this is fairly simple. The yearly figure is simply divided by the square root of whatever time is under investigation, and this result is multiplied by the stock price.

In the above example the stock being investigated had a yearly volatility of 25%, but what if we are interested in the monthly volatility of this stock? To calculate this we simply divide the yearly volatility by the square root of 12 (number of months) and multiply by $5.00. Hence the monthly volatility would be:

$$(0.25 \div \sqrt{12}) \times \$5.00 = (0.25 \div 3.46) \times \$5.00 = \$0.36$$

So in the period under question we could expect the stock to be within the range of $4.64 to $5.36 on 2 out of 3 occasions. Such knowledge is extremely important when it comes to picking options to trade.

If at this stage you are a little confused by all of this, *don't panic.* I will show you how to automate this process.

Step 4 – A Little Help

As I said, this process can be automated so that all you really have to worry about is putting the volatility figure into an options pricing model. I will look now at a few freely available tools.

Volatility can be calculated automatically using a variety of packages, such as SuperCharts or MetaStock. When using such a package, volatility is displayed as an indicator. It is then a simple matter of reading the current value and entering that figure into the options pricing equation. It can also be calculated with Microsoft Excel, which has included with it a statistical analysis package. However, this method is rather laborious and will require access to daily price data that will need to be manually entered into Excel.

The Australian Stock Exchange also publishes a list of its estimates of the historical volatilities of stocks. These can be downloaded from the following address:

www.asx.com.au/markets/pdf/Clm10701.pdf

Having generated a volatility figure by whatever method you have access to, it is then simply a matter of entering that figure into a pricing calculator. If you have either SuperCharts or MetaStock then this calculator is included in your charting package.

Free calculators are available from:

www.hoadley.net/options/options.htm

www.cboe.com/TradTool/OptionCalculator.asp

As an example, consider Figure 2.17 (overleaf). This is a calculator designed by Peter Hoadley. This calculator is extremely simple to use. All it requires are the standard Black-Scholes inputs. (For the sake of simplicity I have chosen a non-dividend paying example.)

Once the figures are entered, the calculator will generate a range of prices for the option under certain price conditions. It will then map this in a simple payoff diagram.

Step 5 – Why Use Volatility?

The easy answer to this is that we need a volatility figure to make the pricing equation work. But, as we will see, such an answer is too superficial. Much of the work regarding option trading is centred around approximations of historical volatility, and it is historical volatility that we have been examining. We have been looking back at the trading history of a stock and making a judgement of the level of volatility that has been observed.

However, the question remains as to why volatility is so important, apart from simply giving us a figure to enter into an equation. Part of the answer lies in the way option pricing equations use volatility. Volatility determines the chances of an option reaching a certain point. This likely outcome is plugged into the option's price equation to generate a price for the option.

Figure 2.17 *Hoadley Web-Based Price Calculator*

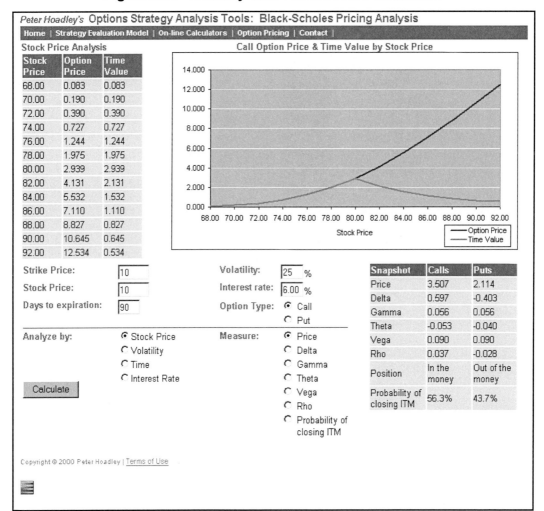

Reproduced with the permission of Peter Hoadley.

Volatility is the single most important component of option pricing. It is important because it is not directly observable, and changes in the level of underlying volatility can dramatically impact on the price of a given option. In turn this will influence the type of strategy that is employed.

The relationship between an option price and volatility is linear, therefore a change in volatility will have a dramatic impact upon an option. Consider Figure 2.18. This chart simply tracks the impact of volatility upon an at-the-money 1000 call with 90 days till expiry. As can be seen, changing the volatility greatly influences the price of the option. Lift the volatility and the price of the option lifts, drop the volatility and the option price falls. It is that simple.

Figure 2.18 *Changes in Volatility Vs Option Price*

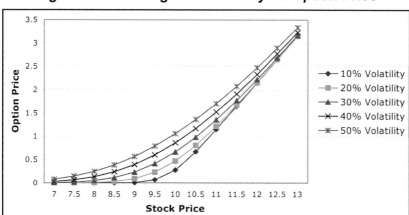

As an example consider a trader who had bought a call with the same terms shown in the chart above. Imagine that this trader had bought the option when volatility was 50%, and suddenly volatility dropped to 10%. The value of this option would be slashed without the underlying stock moving at all. This will happen to most option traders at some stage. To give a practical demonstration of what can happen with volatility, watch the price of the calls and puts as derived by the Chicago Board Options Exchange calculator (below and on the following page) as the volatility is dropped from 50% to 10%.

Figure 2.19 *CBOE Option Calculator – 50% Volatility*

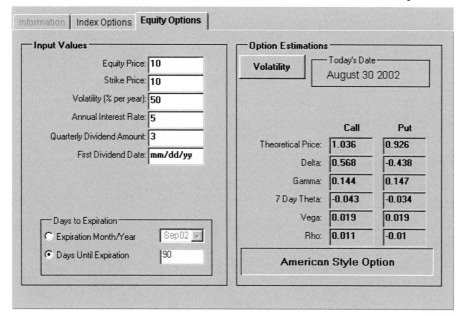

Figure 2.20   CBOE Option Calculator – 10% Volatility

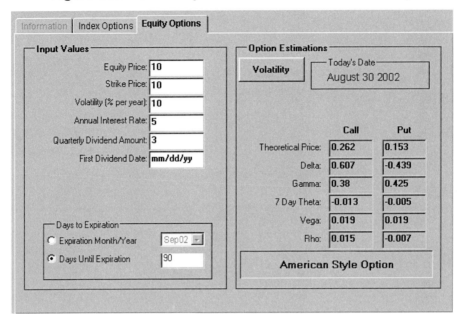

Provided as a courtesy by Chicago Board Options Exchange, Incorporated.

The calls are valued at $1.03, the puts are valued at 92¢. Now without changing any of the variables other than volatility observe what happens to the price of the options.

The value of the calls and puts has imploded, so with no change in any variable other than volatility any trader who was long either of those options would now be faced with a disaster.

Step 6 – Relevance to Trading

To fully explore the impact of volatility upon trading it is necessary to introduce two new concepts: implied volatility and mean reversion.

I will start with the concept of mean reversion. Put simply, all activity reverts to a mean value. As an example consider how a thermostat works. The temperature that you set the thermostat to can be considered the mean. The heating system will heat the room until the temperature overshoots the required temperature, the mean. The heating then switches itself off. As the room cools the temperature drops below the set temperature and the heater switches itself on again.

An example of this in the stock market can be found in the use of moving averages. A moving average is effectively a mean consensus of the value of the stock as defined by the closing price taken over a number of days. An example is shown opposite.

Figure 2.21 *ANZ with Moving Average*

Notice how price oscillates around the moving average. Price will travel a certain distance away from the moving average and then retrace its steps back to the moving average. It will then make another excursion away from the moving average, only to be drawn back.

Historical volatility displays this capacity for mean reversion. There is an average volatility for any period being examined, and the historical volatility will oscillate around this. This can be seen in Figure 2.22 (overleaf).

The second concept I want to explore is implied volatility. When we are faced with the task of pricing an option we are required to input a series of variables, the most important of which is the estimation of volatility. This estimation of volatility is made with regard to the underlying share.

However, consider a situation where we enter all the variables and arrive at a theoretical price for an option of 50¢. Having done our calculation, we then check our quote screen and see that this option is trading at 65¢. We believe it is worth 50¢ yet the market believes it is worth 65¢. How do we account for such a radical difference?

The answer to this requires us to look at the variables in the pricing equation. It is unlikely that we would have the time to expiry, exercise price or the price of the underlying wrong.

Figure 2.22 *ANZ Historical Volatility*

The only other two variables are interest rates and volatility. As was explained earlier interest rates are a minor influence on the price of an option. Minor variations in the accepted figure for the risk-free rate would not produce wild perturbations in an option's price. Therefore this leaves volatility as the variable which the market disagrees over.

It is possible to restructure the option pricing equation so that it can calculate the market's interpretation of volatility. Such an approach requires the entering of the current market price for the option.

To illustrate how easily this can be done consider the spreadsheet opposite. In the first column I have entered all the option details but I have left the volatility row empty. In the second column I have entered the option's current market price and simply asked the spreadsheet to solve for the volatility.

With a tool such as this it is very easy for traders to generate implied volatility figures. Such tools are readily available. This particular version was included in the SuperCharts charting package. A similar tool is included in MetaStock.

If you do not have access to either of these charting packages there are online tools available from www.cboe.com. Some information delivery systems will also provide implied volatility figures.

Asset Sym	BHP	BHP
Option Sym		
Model	Equity ▼	Equity ▼
Rate	5.5	5.5
Dividend	0.00	0.00
Calc Date	08/31/01	08/31/01
Exp Date	11/30/01	11/30/01
Strike	10.0000	10.0000
Underlying	10.0000	10.0000
Option Type	Long Call ▼	Long Cal ▼
Option Price	0.0000	0.5000
Volatility	0.0000	21.6600
Delta	0.0000	0.5718
Gamma	0.0000	0.3629
Theta	0.0000	-0.0033
Vega	0.0000	0.0194
Days Left	0	91

The importance of being able to generate both historical and implied volatility figures and their application to trading will be further examined when we look at trading methodologies.

Summary

Option pricing is not as difficult as some would make out. Granted there are quantitative analysts who spend their lives refining pricing methodologies, and in the years following the release of the Black-Scholes formula there have been numerous variations.

Our job, however, is not to be an expert on option pricing but rather to understand how a change in each of the components of an option's price will influence our trading decisions.

The contents of this chapter can largely be summarised into the following table. My advice to traders who think they may struggle with option pricing is not to panic, but rather understand the broad facts about pricing and let the freely available technology do all the work. What you must commit to memory though is the table on the following page.

Changing input variables	Effect on Calls	Effect on Puts
Underlying increases in value	Increase	Decrease
Underlying decreases in value	Decrease	Increase
Time to expiry decreases	Decrease	Decrease
Dividend increase	Decrease	Increase
Dividend decrease	Increase	Decrease
Interest rate increase	Increase	Decrease
Interest rate decrease	Decrease	Increase
Volatility increase	Increase	Increase
Volatility decrease	Decrease	Decrease

Answer: Both charts on page 30 were generated randomly.

This chapter is an extract from Christopher Tate's Option Trader Home Study Course.

3

Option Sensitivities

By the end of this chapter you should be able to:

- ▲ Identify the major option sensitivities.
- ▲ Define the changes measured by each sensitivity.
- ▲ Identify the impact of each sensitivity upon an option trading strategy.

Sensitivity Analysis

As we have already seen, there are a wide variety of factors that influence an option's price. As a result, option trading is extremely fluid and dynamic.

As the variables change, so does the price of an option. For example, each change in the underlying share price alters a trader's risk/reward profile in either a positive way or a negative way. It is therefore essential that traders be completely aware of how changing conditions will affect their option positions. However, understanding the significance of changes in different factors can be quite difficult.

To simplify the task it is necessary to introduce a number of 'option sensitivities', which are represented by the Greek names delta, gamma, theta and vega. They are often simply referred to as 'the Greeks'. Each of these is a measurement of the correlation between an option's trading price and one of the variables which influences it. They calculate how sensitive an option's price is to variables such as the price of the underlying share, interest rates and the passing of time, enabling traders to easily recognise the risks faced by any given option position, and to assess the effects of changes in these variables.

Delta

Delta is the most widely known option sensitivity. It is defined as the amount an option price will move either up or down for a given change in the underlying share price.

Call option deltas are always positive and they are measured in a range from 0.0 to 1.0. The upper boundary of a call option delta is always 1.0 because the option theoretically cannot increase at a greater rate than the underlying share. The lower boundary is 0.0 because the call cannot have a negative value.

A deep in-the-money call option with a delta of 1.0 will increase at the rate of one full tick for every full tick move in the underlying share price. For example, if we were trading an NCP call which had a delta of 1.0 then when NCP increased by 1¢ our call option would also increase by 1¢. Likewise should NCP fall by 1¢ then the call option would fall by 1¢.

A deep out-of-the-money call with a delta of, for example, 0.1, will only move 0.1 of a cent for every 1¢ move made by the underlying share. As a rule of thumb, very deep in-the-money calls will have a delta very close to 1.0, at-the-money calls will have a delta of approximately 0.5 and out-of-the-money calls will have deltas that move toward 0.0 the further out-of-the-money they become.

Figure 3.1 illustrates the standard delta curve for a call option.

Figure 3.1 *Call Option Delta*

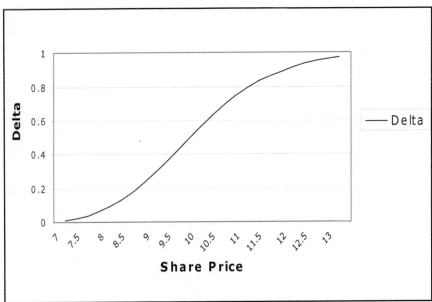

Those of you familiar with calculus have probably realised that all the delta does is measure the slope of the change in an option price. In maths speak it is the slope of the line drawn tangent to the option price curve.

Delta and Time

It is important to realise that deltas are not constant. Any change in the time until expiry will result in a change in the delta and this change will be different depending upon whether the option is in-the-money, at-the-money or out-of-the-money. Figure 3.2 illustrates the change in delta for an at-the-money option with varying times to expiry.

Figure 3.2 *Call Option Delta Vs Time till Expiry*

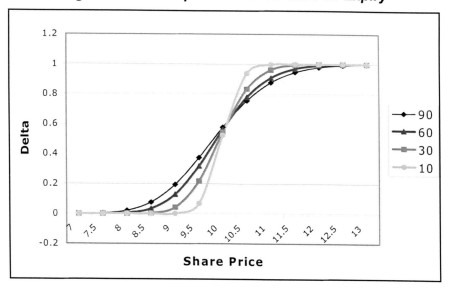

In Figure 3.2 the deltas for options with 10, 30, 60 and 90 days to expiry are compared. As can be seen an option's delta will also vary depending upon the amount of time till expiry. As a general rule, the delta of an out-of-the-money call option falls dramatically as the expiry date approaches. This reflects the low probability of this particular option finishing in-the-money, whereas the in-the-money option has a delta that approaches 1.0 since the probability of this option remaining in-the-money at expiry is high.

To date we have only discussed call option deltas. As you would expect, put option deltas function exactly the same way except in reverse. Put option deltas are measured from 0.0 to −1.0. The same general guidelines apply; deep in-the-money puts will have deltas approaching −1.0, at-the-money puts will have deltas approaching −0.5 and out-of-the-money puts will have deltas ranging from −0.5 to 0.0.

Why Use Delta?

One reason delta is often referred to is that it gives an approximate percentage chance of an option finishing in-the-money. For example if an option has a delta of 0.5 then it has about a 50% chance of finishing in-the-money. Such a concept does not really stand up to any sort of vigorous testing though, since it disregards any directional risk. As such it is of limited use.

Delta is useful in that it enables traders to gain an understanding of how an option will respond to a move in the underlying share. It also enables us to think in terms of share equivalency. Most traders who begin options trading have graduated from trading equities, so their thinking is geared towards the risks inherent in equities trading. The natural consequence of this is that there is a period of adjustment while they attune themselves to the risks involved in options trading. Fortunately the concept of delta can help ease this transition.

For example, if we were long ten BHP-Billiton Oct 1000 calls which had a delta of 0.65 then we would have an equivalent stock position of 6,500 BHP-Billiton (delta of 0.65 × 10 contracts). Naturally we would like to see this position gain in value, because if BHP-Billiton increases in value then the option should see an increase in its delta value. So, if the delta increases to 0.75 we would then have an equivalent share position of 7,500 BHP-Billiton shares. If the delta were to drop to 0.40 we would only be in control of 4,000 BHP-Billiton shares. Such a move would indicate that the underlying share was moving against our position and our option was moving further out-of-the-money.

I need to issue a warning here. Many traders assume that delta is the only measure of directional risk for options trading. This is a false assumption. Gamma is referred to as the true measure of directional risk in options trading.

Gamma

Gamma is defined as the rate of change in an option's delta. Consider the situation of an at-the-money call and put option. As the price of the underlying increases the delta of the call approaches 1.0 and the delta of the put approaches 0.0. If the underlying falls then the call option delta moves towards 0.0 and the put option delta moves towards −1.0. The measure of this change in delta is called gamma.

All gammas are positive in their influence upon delta. For example, if we had a call option with a delta of 0.50 and a gamma of 0.05 then a one tick increase in the underlying would cause the delta to move to 0.55. Put option gammas are also positive, so if we had a put option with a delta of −0.50 and a gamma of 0.05 then a one tick move up in the underlying share would mean that the delta would become −0.45. This may seem somewhat confusing, but, put simply, negative 0.50 (the option delta) plus positive 0.05 equals negative 0.45 (the new delta). Such a move in gamma reflects that the option is moving further out-of-the-money as the underlying share moves in a bullish direction. If the underlying share were to fall by a tick then the gammas would be subtracted from the delta, so the call delta would move to 0.45 (0.50 – 0.05) and the put delta would become –0.55 (–0.50 – 0.05). This also makes sense because the calls would be moving further out-of-the-money and the put would be moving further into the money.

Why Use Gamma?

Since gamma is the rate of change in delta, the higher the gamma the greater the acceleration in delta. This is an important point for option buyers since we want to get the maximum bang for our bucks. We want the rate of acceleration in the change in the option value to be as high as possible. If we get maximum gamma then when the stock starts to move, hopefully in the direction we want, we will get a rapid rise in the option price. This will increase our chances of making a profit from our position.

It should now be apparent that an important question for options traders is "Where can the highest gamma be found?" Options that are deep in-the-money will have a delta of either 1.0 or –1.0 depending on whether they are puts or calls. Hence a change in the price of the underlying will influence the delta of these options. A similar situation exists for options that are deep out-of-the-money. Therefore the highest gamma values are to be found in options that are at-the-money. To test this hypothesis it is possible to map an option's gamma.

Consider Figure 3.3, which displays the curvature of gamma as an option moves into the money.

Figure 3.3 *Option Gamma Curve*

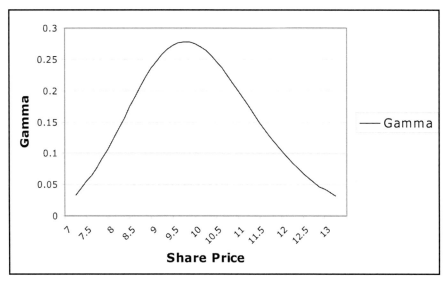

Option gamma is highest in the vicinity of at-the-money, therefore if we were an option buyer this is the area from which we would start selecting options to buy. Conversely, if we were an option writer we would usually seek to stay away from this region.

To find the option with the highest gamma is a simple matter. Most professional information delivery systems include gamma as a measure in their option quote facilities.

Figure 3.4 shows a typical spreadsheet showing option information (in this case for NCP), with gamma highlighted. It shows options with various strike prices and differing expiry dates. The 'C' after the strike price signifies call options.

Figure 3.4 *Option Spreadsheet*

| | | | | | | | | Derived Values | | | | |
	Expiry	Strike	Bid	Ask	Last	Vol	OpInt	ImpV	Delta	Gamma (%)	Theta	Vega
NCPK3	Jun02	0.01C	0	0	0	0	0	0	0	**0**	0	0
NCPTG	Jun02	10.5C	0.98	1.055	1.255	30	23	49	89.2	**9.9**	-0.011	0.003
NCPTH	Jun02	11C	0.56	0.63	0.8	20	197	45	74.5	**22.6**	-0.017	0.005
NCPEL	Jun02	11.5C	0.27	0.29	0.315	415	579	43	49.8	**40.5**	-0.02	0.007
NCPXH	Jun02	12C	0.11	0.12	0.12	169	1377	44	25.9	**47.2**	-0.016	0.006
NCPEF	Jun02	12.5C	0.03	0.055	0.05	238	963	46	11.4	**38.8**	-0.009	0.003
NCPEG	Jun02	13C	0.02	0.035	0.035	53	3502	55	6.9	**25.3**	-0.007	0.002
NCPEH	Jun02	13.5C	0.005	0.015	0.015	129	3982	56	2.8	**15.4**	-0.004	0.001
NCPEI	Jun02	14C	0	0.005	0.005	99	2662	55	0.8	**7.7**	-0.001	0
NCPEK	Jun02	14.5C	0	0	0	0	2794	0	0	**0**	0	0
NCPEO	Jun02	15C	0	0	0	0	589	0	0	**0**	0	0
NCPQ1	Jul02	0.01C	0	0	0	0	90	0	0	**0**	0	0
NCPQJ	Jul02	10.5C	1.22	1.3	1.26	0	8	45	76.3	**14**	-0.008	0.011
NCPQM	Jul02	11C	0.885	0.915	0.945	12	91	43	65.8	**18.9**	-0.009	0.013
NCPQB	Jul02	11.5C	0.6	0.635	0.61	36	447	42	53.2	**22.9**	-0.009	0.014
NCPQE	Jul02	12C	0.4	0.425	0.48	124	605	42	40.5	**24.5**	-0.009	0.014
NCPQG	Jul02	12.5C	0.26	0.275	0.32	46	1740	42	29.5	**23.8**	-0.008	0.012
NCPQH	Jul02	13C	0.15	0.175	0.18	7	634	42	20.2	**21.5**	-0.006	0.01
NCPQI	Jul02	13.5C	0.1	0.11	0.12	10	1643	43	13.9	**17.8**	-0.005	0.008
NCPQO	Jul02	14C	0	0	0.09	11	257	0	0	**0**	0	0
NCPQP	Jul02	14.5C	0	0	0.045	27	439	0	0	**0**	0	0

Since gamma decreases as an option moves deeper into the money this has ramifications for our follow up trades. When we are in a trade that is successful the question arises as to how long do we hold a given option before moving to a new strike price.

To consider how we might use gamma to assist in our trade selection consider Figure 3.5.

Figure 3.5 *ANZ Daily Chart*

During the period under consideration ANZ was in a continual uptrend. Imagine that at the beginning of the uptrend we had bought a long-dated 1350 call, so that time decay was not an issue. Our judgement is proved correct and the stock begins to move upward.

As the uptrend continues we are faced with a dilemma; do we simply hold the option we originally purchased or do we chase the trend by moving to a higher strike price? Mapping the gamma curves of several options provides us with an answer.

Figure 3.6 (overleaf) plots the gamma of a series of options through a range of underlying share prices. What it indicates is that holding the original position as the share price increased would not have been the most efficient means of trading this sustained move.

As the option moves in-the-money, the gamma of the option begins to fall rapidly whereas the gamma of the next strike price is still increasing. In effect there is a gamma wave that traders need to be able to surf. The point at which an option position should be rolled is at the intersection of the two gamma curves. So when the gamma of the 1350 falls below that of the 1400 the 1350 should be closed down and the position moved.

Figure 3.6 *Gamma Curves*

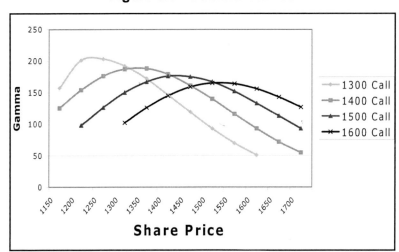

You should note that all this is being done with the value of hindsight—a trader in this position would not have known with any degree of certainty how long the trend would last.

Remember that the prime rule of trading is to follow the trend. If the trend is up and you have a bullish position then you should have in place strategies to enable you to extract as much profit as is safely possible from the move. One of the main reasons why traders fail is that they simply refuse to allow their profits to run whereas they allow their loses to accelerate and eventually ruin them. The psychological reasons why this occurs are beyond the scope of this book but you must be aware of the need to maximise your profits and minimise your losses. (For information on the psychology of trading, you can refer to one of my other books, *The Art of Trading*.)

The concept of gamma can also be used to help with risk management. It can do this in two ways. The first relates to gamma rolling and the second to a concept we touched on in the section on delta—equivalent share positions.

Let's return to the above example of the uptrend in ANZ and assume that instead of having a bullish position we have a written call option at 1300. Such a position is bearish and, as you will recall, written options have limited profit potential and unlimited risk.

There is a school of thought, particularly among option advisers, that written positions which become dangerous should simply be rolled to a higher strike price and a more distant expiry date. So in the example of our written call we would simply buy back the 1350 call (presumably at a loss) and attempt to recoup the loss by writing a larger number of contracts at $14.00 with a later expiry date. There is a problem, however, posed by rolling written positions during a period of a sharp upward move—the problem of increasing volatility.

Figure 3.7 displays the lift in volatility of ANZ shares towards the end of the uptrend.

Figure 3.7 *ANZ Volatility Increase*

There is an important point to highlight about volatility. It is quite possible for a share to trend very strongly yet display no increase in volatility. This is the situation in the early part of the ANZ chart. Remember from Chapter 2, trend and volatility are not the same.

Increasing volatility will increase option prices, so any written position will be severely damaged by increasing volatility. Rolling the position will only guarantee a larger loss.

Gamma can also help by giving traders an idea of how their exposure in terms of the underlying share is changing. As discussed in the section on delta, traders who make the transition to trading options often have difficulty coming to terms with the risks inherent in options trading.

For example, consider the trader who was short a call. Traders who are short options are also said to be short gamma, therefore a rise in gamma is harmful to the short position. To understand how quickly a rise in gamma can harm a position, simply convert the options position to a quantity of shares.

Assume that we have written ten call options and that these have a delta of 0.45 and a gamma of 0.05. Effectively this means we are short 4,500 shares (0.45 × 10 contracts). This may be a level of exposure that we are happy with. Based upon our market analysis we may consider being short 4,500 shares to be well within our acceptable level of risk. However, watch what happens to our exposure when the delta starts to move as a result of gamma.

Original position 4,500 shares, delta 0.45, gamma 0.05

1 tick move up in the underlying, delta 0.50, share exposure = 5,000

2 tick move up in the underlying, delta 0.55, share exposure = 5,500

3 tick move up in the underlying, delta 0.60, share exposure = 6,000

4 tick move up in the underlying, delta 0.65, share exposure = 6,500

In the space of a four tick move our equivalent share position has moved from being short 4,500 shares to being short 6,500 shares—a gain of 44%. So a simple move in the underlying has dramatically changed our risk profile. It is for this reason that gamma is referred to as the true measure of directional risk in options trading.

Gamma and Time

Time decay can have a dramatic effect upon an option's gamma. As the time to expiry approaches 0.0, deep in-the-money options will have deltas that approximate 1.0 and movement in the underlying will have less and less impact upon the options' delta. For options that are deep out-of-the-money their delta will approximate 0.0 and their delta will be less and less influenced by changes in the price of the underlying.

The situation for the at-the-money options is somewhat different since the delta will oscillate as the options become either more in-the-money or more out-of-the-money. If the option drifts in-the-money close to expiry then its delta will become larger than if it had a longer time to expiry. The reverse happens if the option becomes out-of-the-money; the delta will shrink to reflect the greater likelihood that the option will finish out-of-the-money and therefore expire worthless.

Figure 3.8 reflects the dramatic difference that time until expiry has upon an option's gamma.

The Importance of Gamma

As we have seen, gamma is the measure of directional risk for an option. Changes in gamma will dictate how dramatically the option will behave in response to changes in the underlying. It is therefore important that traders assess the gamma risk of their positions. If we are short options then we are short gamma. Short option positions are also referred to as having negative gamma. If we are short gamma we do not want gamma to increase. An increase in gamma means that our trade is going bad and we need to take follow-up action such as shutting the trade down.

Figure 3.8 *Gamma vs Time to Expiry*

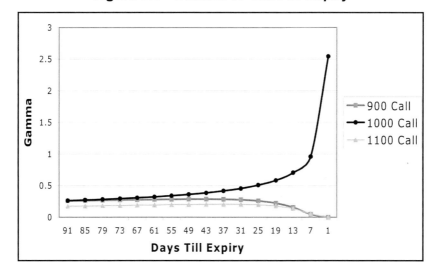

If we are long options then we are long gamma and we want gamma to increase. We are said to have a positive gamma. An increase in gamma will mean that the trade is going in the right direction but only to a point. Gamma will start to fall once the option has moved into the money. If our perception of the direction of the underlying continues to hold true then it is necessary for us to move our options position in the direction of the trend.

Theta

Options are wasting assets. All other factors being constant an option will lose value every day until expiry. The rate of this decay is termed theta and it is expressed as the number of cents lost per day. Technically theta is a positive number, but for the sake of convention and for the reinforcement of the notion that time is running out it is expressed as a negative number. So, if I have an option that today is worth $0.65 and theta is –0.05, then tomorrow if all other factors remain constant it will be worth $0.60.

Long option positions are said to have a negative theta. Notice this is the opposite of gamma. A long option position has a positive gamma. So if I have a bought option I have positive gamma and negative theta. My reward is that gamma may increase due to movement of the underlying share, my risk is my rate of time decay or my theta. I face the risk that time may run out before the market has had an opportunity to move.

Short option positions are said to have a positive theta since they benefit from time decay. As we saw earlier, the aim of option writing is to get time to work for you so that the options expire worthless. However, if I am positive theta then, by definition, I also have a negative gamma. The risk to an option writer is a dramatic change in gamma brought about by a sudden move in the underlying whereas the reward is that time is passing. As each day passes the effect of time decay accelerates.

Just as at-the-money options had the highest gamma, the same is also true for theta. An option that is at-the-money will have the greatest rate of time decay.

Vega

As was mentioned in Chapter 2, volatility is the prime driver in option trading. A failure to understand volatility will result in catastrophic losses throughout your option trading career. Vega is the measurement of the sensitivity of an option's price to a point change in the prevailing level of volatility. Since all long options rise in value when volatility increases, vega is positive.

The concept of a change in volatility is a very important one since it requires us to make a judgement as to which of the volatilities vega is referring to. This question can be answered quite easily. In Chapter 2 we looked at historical and implied volatility. Implied volatility is the market's current perception of volatility. Vega refers to a change in this current perception.

When comparing options with the same expiry date, vega is higher amongst the at-the-money options. An example of this is shown in Figure 3.9, in which the 1000 call is closest to being at-the-money. Vega is lower in both in-the-money and out-of-the-money options. Such options are relatively less influenced by changes in volatility.

Figure 3.9 *Option Vega vs Time to Expiry*

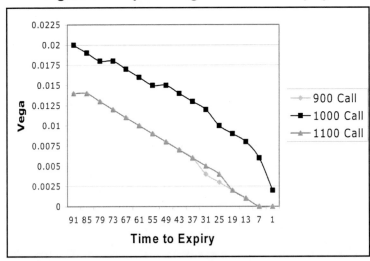

Volatility and time are closely associated. As shown by Figure 3.10, the more time to expiry, the greater the potential uncertainty. Time equals uncertainty. The greater the time to expiry the more chance there is for a given event to occur. Increasing time is equivalent to increasing volatility. Decreasing time is equivalent to decreasing volatility.

Figure 3.10 *Vega vs Time Till Expiry*

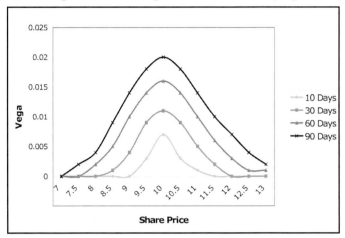

The option with the greatest time to expiry will show the greatest vega. This is merely a reflection of the fact that there is more time for any number of possible events to occur. These events are all capable of influencing the price of an option. Think of time as room to manoeuvre; the more time, the more potential for a move in any given direction. The less time, the less potential for a move. Given that vega is a measure of the change in an option price for a given change in volatility, it is necessary to understand how changes in volatility influence vega, an example of which is shown in Figure 3.11.

Figure 3.11 *Vega vs Volatility*

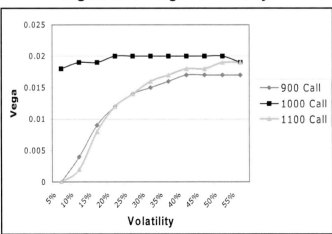

The vega of at-the-money options is relatively insensitive to changes in volatility. Such a lack of sensitivity allows us to make stable assumptions regarding how an at-the-money option will perform under a wide variety of volatility conditions.

Quick Revision

Delta

▶ Measures the relationship between a change in the price of an underlying instrument and the change in the price of the option.

▶ Call options have a positive delta that is measured from 0.0 to 1.0. Deep in-the-money call options have a delta approximating 1.0, at-the-money call options have an approximate delta of 0.5 and out-of-the-money call options have a delta ranging from 0.5 to 0.0.

▶ Put options have a negative delta that is measured from 0.0 to −1.0. Deep in-the-money put options have a delta approximating −1.0, at-the-money put options have a delta of approximately −0.5 and out-of-the-money put options have a delta ranging from −0.5 to 0.0.

Gamma

▶ Is referred to as a second derivative of price. It measures the rate of change in an option's delta for a given move in the underlying instrument.

▶ At-the-money options have the highest gamma.

▶ Gamma is the true measure of directional risk faced by traders.

Theta

▶ Is a measure of the rate at which an option's time value is decaying.

▶ Theta is always greatest for at-the-money options.

▶ A long-dated at-the-money option will always have a lower theta value than a short-dated at-the-money option.

Vega

▶ Is a measure of how an option's price will change with a change in the underlying volatility.

▶ At-the-money options have the greatest vega in absolute terms.

▶ The vega of at-the-money options is relatively insensitive to changes in volatility. The vega of all options will decrease as the time to expiry draws near.

The Greeks and Trading

So far we have only looked at the Greeks in isolation. We have simply defined their impact and made a few judgements as to where their influence will be most strongly felt. However each option strategy has a unique population of Greeks and this population will tell you how an option strategy will vary under any given set of conditions.

In Chapter 1, we saw that there are six basic strategies. They are:

1. Buy the underlying stock.

2. Short sell the underlying stock.

3. Buy a call (long call).

4. Sell a call (short call).

5. Buy a put (long put).

6. Sell a put (short put).

All option strategies are assembled from these basic components and each of these components contributes a given Greek to a strategy.

Table 3.1 *Strategies and the Greeks*

Strategy	Delta is	Gamma is	Theta is	Vega is
Long the underlying	positive	0	0	0
Short the underlying	negative	0	0	0
Long calls	positive	positive	negative	positive
Short calls	negative	negative	positive	negative
Long puts	negative	positive	negative	positive
Short puts	positive	negative	positive	negative

To decipher the above table it is necessary to think in terms of what you are hoping will occur with any given strategy. For example, if I own a basket of shares then my delta is positive and must be 1.0. I don't have to worry about gamma since my delta will never be any more or any less than 1.0. I suffer no time decay since theoretically a share can be held forever, and any change in the underlying volatility will not have an impact upon a basket of shares.

The situation is somewhat different if I own a call option. If I own a call, I am bullish in my view. I want the stock to rise, hence the delta to increase. I am positive gamma so I want a swift move in a positive direction. As a call option buyer, time is my enemy so I am negative theta. Time passing hurts my position. I also want an increase in volatility since a volatility increase will impact positively upon my calls.

Each Greek also has a favoured outcome. For example if I am positive vega I want the underlying level of volatility to increase, irrespective of whether I own puts or calls. The preferred outcome for each strategy can be easily summarised as follows:

Table 3.2 *Preferred Outcome*

Position	Preferred Outcome
Positive delta	Rise in price of underlying
Negative delta	Fall in price of underlying
Positive gamma	Strong move in any direction
Negative gamma	Sluggish move in any direction
Positive theta	Time passing will increase the value of the position
Negative theta	Time passing will decrease the value of the position
Positive vega	Increasing volatility
Negative vega	Fall in volatility

When we look at strategies in further chapters the Greeks will be examined for their influence upon given market views.

Finding the Greeks

To date I have talked about the theoretical aspects of the Greeks, what they measure and how they can be used to describe preferred outcomes for various strategies. I now want to focus on the more practical aspect of finding relevant values for the Greeks.

Finding and/or calculating the Greeks is a relatively easy process and can be done quite inexpensively in many instances.

The first online calculator I want to look at is provided by Peter Hoadley at www.hoadley.net/options/options.htm. This site provides a range of calculators based upon various pricing models. (If you are trading a dividend-paying stock—and the vast majority of Australian ETOs are based upon stocks that pay dividends—then it is essential you find a dividend calendar. I have already mentioned the location of one such calendar at www.egoli.com.)

Figure 3.12   *Online Calculator*

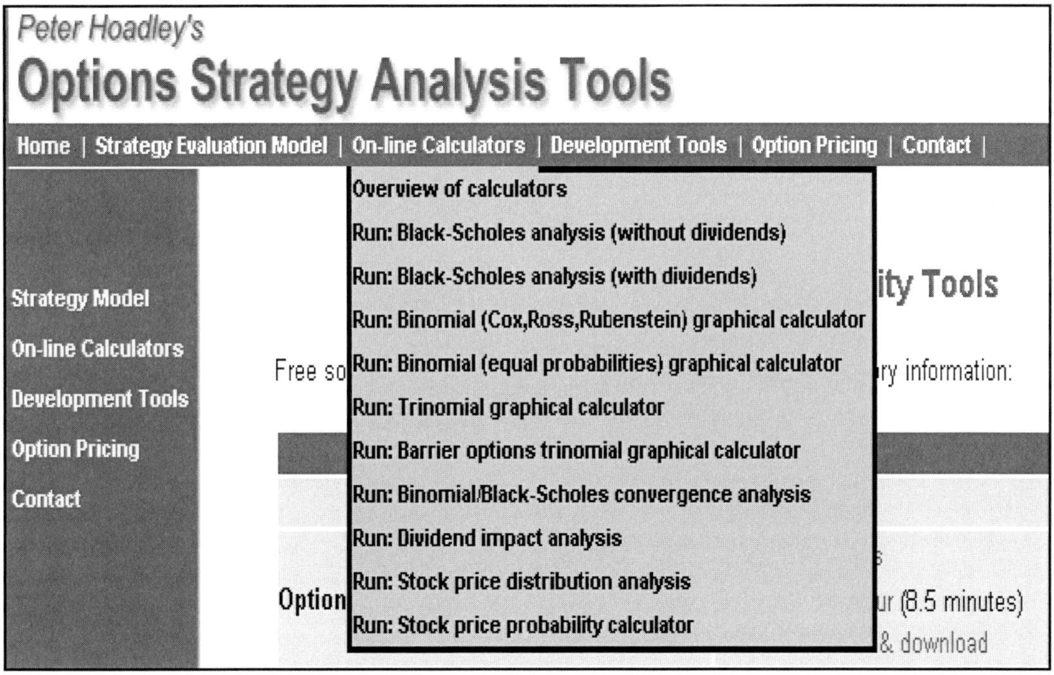

These images are reproduced with the permission of Peter Hoadley.

The Hoadley calculators are simple-to-use, web-based applications. The page opens with a list of alternative destinations, and as you would expect, the calculators are located under the 'On-line Calculators' heading.

For the sake of ease I have chosen the Black-Scholes (non-dividend) model. Once a model is chosen a simple window opens and gives you the opportunity to choose the variables you wish to measure. For this example (overleaf) I have chosen a 8000 call option with 30 days until expiry, an interest rate of 6.00% and a historical volatility of 30%. The price of the underlying has been set at $81.00.

Figure 3.13 *Sensitivity Analysis*

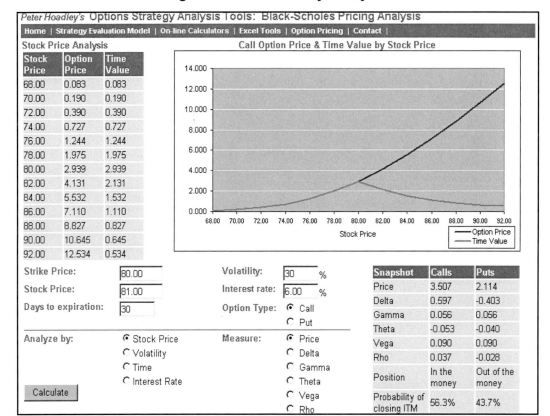

The resultant screen enables you not only to calculate but also to graph the Greeks. The advantages of the Hoadley web-based application are that it is free, very comprehensive and easy to use. Its only disadvantages are that it is not geared directly to an information source, so inputs such as 'time to expiry' have to be entered manually, and you cannot generate values for a chain of options simultaneously.

Another useful calculator can be found at the ASX website, at www.asx.com.au/options. Once you select the option calculator, the option you wish to examine is then selected from the drop down menu. Once you have selected your underlying security or index you will be taken to the screen shown in Figure 3.14, from which you select the option series you wish to examine. This will lead to the information shown in Figure 3.15.

This screen is extremely useful since it already has details entered for date of expiry, date and amount of dividends, underlying price, theoretical option price, implied volatility for the theoretical price and historic volatility.

Figure 3.14 *ASX Option Pricing Website*

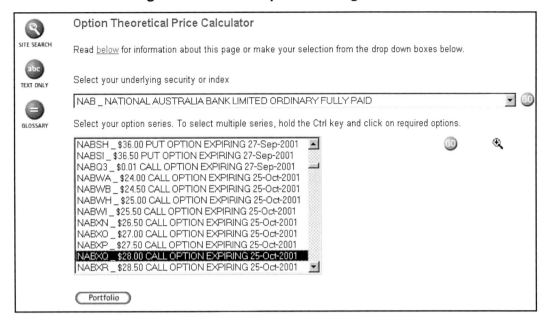

Figure 3.15 *NAB Call Price Analysis*

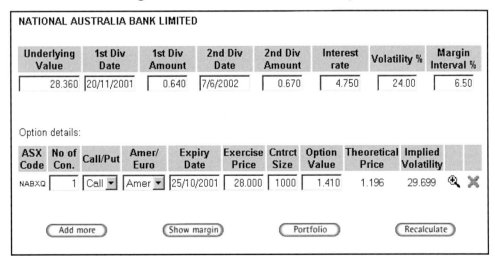

Clicking on the small spyglass next to the figure for implied volatility will yield the screen shown in Figure 3.16.

Figure 3.16 *NAB Sensitivity Analysis*

NATIONAL AUSTRALIA BANK LIMITED

Date Value (today)	Underlying Value	Interest Rate	Volatility %	Margin Interval %	Binomial steps
13/9/2001	28.360	4.750	24.00	6.50	50

1st Div Amount	1st Div Date	2nd Div Amount	2nd Div Date	3rd Div Amount	3rd Div Date	4th Div Amount	4th Div Date	Ann Div Yield
0.640	20/11/2001	0.670	7/6/2002	0.000		0.000		0.000

Option details:

Asx Code	Call/Put	Amer/Euro	Expiry Date	Exercise Price	LastSale Price	Theoretical Price
NABXQ	Call ▾	Amer ▾	25/10/2001	28.000	1.410	1.196

Implied volatility calculation:

Your Price		Implied Volatility :	
1.410			29.699

Option "Greeks":

Delta	Gamma	Theta	Rho	Vega
.6035	.1645	-.0126	3.7330	1.8336

This screen provides all the information required by the option trader. Once again, the only disadvantage is that you cannot examine strings of options simultaneously. Each option must be entered individually.

The other cheap alternative to the free web-based calculators is to use the calculators that come with tools such as MetaStock and SuperCharts. Both these charting packages are equipped with rudimentary options pricing tools, though the tools in both MetaStock and SuperCharts are inferior to the material offered on the Hoadley and ASX websites.

This chapter is an extract from Christopher Tate's Option Trader Home Study Course.

Call Buying

By the end of this chapter you should be able to:

▲ Understand the life cycle of a call option.

▲ Select a call using appropriate selection criteria.

▲ Understand the effects of time.

Just as complex discussions surrounding option pricing models and behaviour have deterred many traders, so too have discussions of option trading strategies. Having weathered the mathematics encountered in the early stages of options texts, the trader is then confronted by such strange beasts as long and short butterflies, put and call ratio backspreads, condors, boxes and conversions.

Yet just as option pricing is, in reality, simple, so too are option strategies. A trader may buy or short sell a share, buy or sell a call or buy or sell a put. The payoff diagram for buying a call was shown in Chapter 1.

As discussed in Chapter 1, it is from these foundations that all options strategies are created, and a trader need only be familiar with these strategies to be a successful participant in the options market. The type and complexity of strategies that can be assembled from these foundations are only limited by how adventurous and imaginative a trader is.

We will start in this chapter with buying calls.

A trader's success in profiting from call buying depends upon picking the right stock and the right call—it is a matter of selection and timing. (Strictly speaking, call buying is not a strategy as such since it does not allow for error or for traders to be neutral in their perception.) This brings us to an important consideration: call buying is very bullish. If you are a call buyer you must be convinced that there will be a sharp upward movement in the price of the underlying stock, and this may or may not coincide with a volatility spike. If the stock goes sideways or down, you will lose your money.

Having said this, why then do traders buy calls? (In Australia in May 2002, some 861,142 calls were traded.) There are three primary reasons why traders buy calls. We will look at these below.

Leverage

For a small outlay in cash, traders can participate in the upward movements in the price of a given stock, which may result in considerable profit. To illustrate this, consider the following comparison between a call buyer and a stock owner:

BHP-Billiton is selling for $10.50   BHP-Billiton July 1000 call is selling for 60¢

Two months later:

BHP-Billiton is selling for $11.50   BHP-Billiton July 1000 call is selling for $1.00

The leverage available in the above situation can be shown as follows.

Table 4.1 *Leverage*

	Option	Stock
Initial cash outlay	$600	$10,500
Sale proceeds	$1,000	$11,500
Profit	$400	$1,000
% Return	66%	9.5%

The leverage that options provide enables traders to gain exposure to numerous sectors of the market for a relatively small outlay. Since all industry groups are represented by option-traded stocks a trader can, within limits, effectively assemble a portfolio of stocks representing a large proportion of the Australian stock market.

Novice option traders often buy deep out-of-the-money calls based on the presumption that they are cheap and offer greater leverage. This shows a poor understanding of the role of gamma and an overconfidence in analysis.

Speculation

This advantage applies equally to both stock owners and those who may only be pure speculators. Suppose that you are a long-term trader with a core portfolio of non-volatile stocks and you wish to participate in a more volatile market sector without the required capital outlay and possibility of subsequent loss.

As an example, assume that you hold 5,000 ANZ shares on a long-term basis, but wish to take advantage of what you perceive to be the high volatility of a stock such as NCP. It is possible to take positions in NCP for a small capital outlay without liquidating your ANZ holding.

Stock Purchase

If we refer to a call as being the right to purchase a given stock at a defined price, then the advantage of call buying in purchasing stock becomes immediately apparent. For example, a trader may want to participate in BHP-Billiton if it breaks key trendlines, which may indicate a strong upward break. In such an instance, BHP-Billiton may be trading at $10.00 and the trader may be willing to participate if it rallies strongly through $10.50. To do so the trader purchases a BHP-Billiton 1050 call. If BHP-Billiton does rally strongly and the call is in-the-money, the trader may choose to exercise the call and acquire the stock. If BHP-Billiton does not increase in value, the trader has not tied up a large proportion of capital and any potential loss is limited to the premium paid for the call.

A natural extension of this may be a trader who does not wish to 'miss the market'. Suppose a trader is rolling out of a cash investment such as a bank bill or certificate of deposit and knows that at a certain date in the future she will have cash available. Yet in the interim this person wishes to participate in a given stock, feeling a rise is imminent. This particular dilemma can be solved by purchasing an appropriate call. If a rise does occur then the call can be exercised and the stock paid for when cash is eventually available.

How to Select a Call

In terms of the Australian Options Market (AOM), a trader's choice of stock is largely restricted due to the limited nature of the market. Despite the presence of market makers, who are compelled to deal in stocks in order to provide liquidity, many stocks, in reality, are notoriously illiquid and traders may find them hard to deal in.

The most popular traded stocks tend to be the major resource stocks such as BHP-Billiton, RIO, and MIM, industrial stocks CSR and Foster's Brewing (FBG), the banks ANZ, NAB, Commonwealth and Westpac, and the media giant Newscorp (NCP).

The option level of activity in a particular stock is defined by open interest. This is a measure of the number of contracts that are outstanding. To use an analogy, open interest is the amount of water we have under our keel.

Table 4.2 shows the most popular option stocks in May 2002.

Table 4.2 *Most Popular Option Stocks (May 2002)*

	Volume	% Option Market	Open interest	Vol/ Open Int.	Share volume for May
TLS	215,532	13.90%	324,419	66.40%	690,271,000
NCP	185,874	12.00%	214,597	86.60%	239,392,000
CBA	124,868	8.10%	75,970	164.40%	120,144,000
NAB	123,814	8.00%	78,477	157.80%	130,173,000
BHP	113,886	7.40%	107,636	105.80%	402,608,000
ANZ	81,580	5.30%	76,457	106.70%	162,460,000
AMP	69,180	4.50%	45,399	152.40%	246,826,000
MIM	64,187	4.20%	92,281	152.40%	89,856,000
RIO	55,883	3.60%	60,231	92.80%	47,856,000
LHG	45,665	3.00%	51,924	87.90%	201,770,000
Top 5	763,974	49.40%	801,099	95.40%	1,582,578,000
Top 10	1,080,469	69.90%	1,127,391	95.80%	2,331,346,000
Market	1,546,154	100.00%	1,830,074	84.50%	6,136,277,000

Such a limited range should not be regarded as a handicap since it helps focus the following selection criteria.

Many traders in choosing a stock do so for technical reasons, such as the breaking of key trendlines. Chartists argue that technical influences are more time-specific and provide a key indicator as to when and if a stock is likely to move. It is said that fundamental factors take a non-specific time to affect share prices and that this influence may occur over a long period of time. It could also be argued that the market may have already priced in all available current and future technical information and that stock and option prices merely reflect this expectation.

Two additional points should be noted. Firstly, just because a stock appears to represent tremendous fundamental value and looks cheap, this is no guarantee that the stock will move. Secondly, many traders believe (strangely enough) that, having taken a position in a stock, the stock is somehow aware of this and will naturally go up. Unfortunately, this is not true—a stock does not have any friends. The most effective method of stock selection is to consider all available information, both technical and volatility-based. This sounds obvious and simple, however traders often handicap themselves by not being fully informed. The best way to acquaint yourself with a stock and its movements is simply to watch it over time.

You can see in Table 4.3 the difference between results at expiry of buying a BHP-Billiton 1000 call and BHP-Billiton 1200 call.

Table 4.3 *Results at Expiry*

BHP-Billiton Price	1000 call value	1200 call value
1000	0	0
1050	50	0
1100	100	0
1150	150	0
1200	200	0
1250	250	50
1300	300	100

Which Call?

It can be considered that out-of-the-money calls offer a potential for greater reward; however, they also offer the greatest risk. Often traders will choose an out-of-the-money call because it is cheaper, but this should never be a deciding factor in choosing which call to buy. For example, assume it is August and BHP-Billiton is selling at $10.50; a trader surveys available calls and decides to purchase an October 1200 call because it is the cheapest and he feels BHP-Billiton will rally in the ensuing months. BHP-Billiton rallies to $11.50 by October.

Clearly, the 1200 call will expire worthless. Consider an alternative strategy. Instead of buying the out-of-the-money call, which will experience a decrease in value even before expiry because of the influence of time decay and a lower gamma, our trader buys a 1000 call. As the option approaches expiry, the in-the-money call will be worth at least $1.50, comprising substantial intrinsic value and whatever time value may remain before expiry.

This brings us to a few general rules. Whereas out-of-the-money calls offer higher risk and higher reward, in-the-money calls will offer less risk and better rewards for a modest gain in the stock price. Out-of-the-money calls will offer greater reward for extreme movements in price. Thus very volatile stocks such as News Corporation which are capable of very rapid price appreciation (and depreciation) may present opportunities for call buyers who wish to buy far out-of-the-money calls. However, traders should be intimately familiar with the impact of both gamma and volatility for deep out-of-the-money options.

In summary, risk/reward considerations and an understanding of option dynamics dictate that traders largely confine their call purchases to either slightly in-the-money calls or at-the-money calls. With these there is less chance of losing their entire equity, since they may recover some funds. The option purchased will generally have some intrinsic value remaining at expiry.

Consider our initial example: if BHP-Billiton had not rallied in price and was still only worth $10.50 then our 1000 call would still be worth 50¢, representing its intrinsic value.

Timing

The certainty with which a trader feels there will be a movement in the stock will also influence the choice of which call to buy.

Perhaps the single most important concept that traders should come to terms with in this chapter is that both call and put options are wasting assets. As stated previously, options are investments with a limited life and their value decreases naturally as they age. It can be considered a general rule that, as options approach expiry, it requires a greater movement in the underlying stock for there to be a corresponding movement in a given option. Traders who are unsure of this should review the section on theta.

Time is an enemy of the option buyer. The only allies an option buyer has are a strongly rallying stock and a dynamic lift in volatility. The astute reader will remember from our earlier discussion on volatility that it is possible for the underlying share to move in the anticipated direction but for volatility to collapse. This contrary move in volatility nullifies any directional move.

If you are certain that there will be a significant movement in the underlying stock in the near term, then it is logical to strive for maximum return and not be concerned about possible losses. Thus, you would buy short-term out-of-the-money calls. However, this decision must be tempered by the knowledge that you would very rarely buy an out-of-the-money option with only a week until expiry. Despite the odds against such a strategy this is the approach of the majority of option traders.

If, on the other hand, you are uncertain as to the timing of any upward movement, then you would buy a longer-term call. Such a situation may arise, say, when you have been correlating the effect of a change in the value of the Australian dollar upon the price of BHP-Billiton. You may be certain that a falling Australian dollar has a positive effect upon the price of BHP-Billiton and that such a fall is imminent, yet you know that anticipating the timing of such falls is almost impossible. Hence, you may decide to purchase a long-dated call in order to participate in the stock for as long as possible yet retain flexibility to compensate for any margin of error. However, this extra flexibility has a cost in terms of the premium you pay. Long-dated call options have substantial time value, so even though you are compensating for the uncertainty of your timing, you are paying a higher premium to do so.

Traders must weigh up the cost of time versus any possible benefit from buying long-dated calls. This decision is also enhanced by the knowledge that the longer-dated options have a higher vega, so any upward move in volatility will be reflected in a rising option price.

All of this should be considered in light of the fact that options are short-term investments. Traders are looking to make money from short-term fluctuations in price.

Selection Criteria Summary

So far, I have outlined a basic set of guidelines that may be used to aid the selection of which calls to buy. In summary, these can be defined as:

Stock Selection—Technical and volatility research, aided by observation of how a stock behaves.

Which Call?—In-the-money options offer moderate reward for less risk and are best used when modest gains are expected. Out-of-the-money options are best employed where large swings in the stock price are expected. Be warned; as with all things, the greater the potential reward the greater the risk. Traders should always keep in mind our discussions about gamma when assessing how far an option may move.

Timing—How certain are you? If totally convinced, go for maximum reward with maximum risk. If you are not so convinced, buy time and stay close to the money. Remember the traders' maxim: preserve your capital. If you lose all your money you can't play any more.

Volatility—What is the likelihood of your selected stock moving at all? What does the history of the stock tell you about its ability to move? Is the option overvalued or undervalued with regard to its volatility?

All of this can be reduced to a single guiding rule—if you buy at-the-money or slightly in-the-money calls on stocks you are familiar with, then you should do well; provided your stock goes up.

This leads me to a note of caution based upon personal observation: the majority of call buyers do not make money due to poor selection criteria.

Call Buying and Cash Instruments

As mentioned earlier, many traders buy call options because of the leverage they provide. For a small cash outlay, traders can take positions in a variety of stocks. This leads to an important consideration: call option buying should be part of an overall investment strategy. Traders should not pour all of their available cash into call options merely because they can gain exposure to a wide variety of stocks. Call options enable traders to maintain a large cash position, with all its inherent stability, whilst still gaining exposure to the stock market.

For example, consider the case of the investor who has $100,000 to trade in stocks. A relatively unsophisticated approach would be to invest the total $100,000 in shares; this would give the trader a fairly diverse portfolio but with heightened market risk, i.e. the risk that the market may collapse. In this event her total capital is at risk. A safer approach may be to invest $90,000 in a cash instrument such as a bank bill; the remaining $10,000 could then be used to gain exposure to the equities market via call buying strategies. Too many new traders are overly enamoured with the possibility of vast returns—as such they pour every cent into the trading of a single market product.

Suppose at the end of the first year our trader has lost entirely the $10,000 that was exposed to the equities market. The net position is that she has still retained the $90,000 plus accrued interest. If we assume an interest rate of 4% per annum, that would leave a cash balance of $93,600.

Many options theorists maintain that this is the most efficient means by which to participate in the options market. Its efficiency as a strategy is undoubted; however, it is dependent upon a trader maintaining a disciplined approach as to what percentage of capital is to be exposed to the options market.

This will be a recurrent theme throughout this book. All options trading, be it simple or complex, will be inefficient without firstly an outlook as to how a stock will perform; secondly, a plan on how to take advantage of this view and finally, a defined escape route should things go wrong. Risk is the guiding principle of all trading.

The long call is the most basic of option strategies. Its limited risk and unlimited profit potential make it an excellent candidate for markets where you expect a strong directional move and or a strong volatility move. Many traders are seduced by the notion that 80% of all options expire worthless so the aim of the game should be to write options. This is not necessarily correct; the name of the game is to apply the correct strategy at the correct time.

Figure 4.1 *Call Buying Selection Summary*

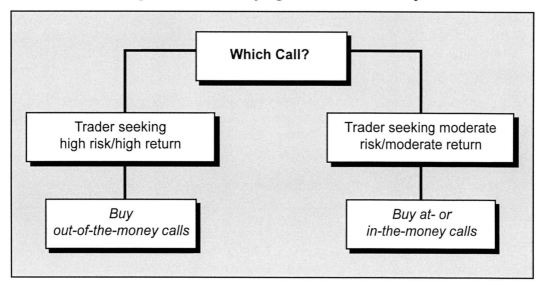

Call Buying Summary

Time Decay: Hurts.

Volatility: Helps.

Potential profit: Profit potential is unlimited in a rising market.

Potential loss: Limited to the premium that was paid. This aspect makes this a good strategy for those who are new to derivatives.

Sensitivity Analysis

Delta: Moves towards 1.0 as the option moves into the money.

Gamma: Gamma falls rapidly as position moves into-the-money or out-of-the-money.

Theta: Time decay will kill this position. From the moment a long call is initiated time is working against it. Theta will accelerate throughout the life of the trade.

Vega: A long call is aided by an increase in volatility. Vega will be greatest for a call that has the longest time to expiry. This is because the greater the length of time the greater the uncertainty, therefore the greater the chance for the underlying to move in any given direction. Vega will also increase as the underlying moves towards the strike price.

What Can Go Wrong

▶ *Poor market analysis.* It is essential to trade in the direction of the trend. Call buying is a strategy designed for strong moves.

▶ *Poor call selection.* New options traders often have poor call selection.

▶ *Not enough time.* Time decay is the enemy of the call. Traders should look to buy time. Buying a call with 14 days remaining is a foolish thing to do.

If It Does Go Wrong

▶ Practise strong money management. Have a defined stop loss point that you will exit at.

▶ It is possible to repair some long call positions. For example, if the market stalls and your perspective goes from strongly bullish to moderately bullish you could turn the position into a bull call spread (see Chapter 8) by selling a higher strike price call. If your view goes from bullish to bearish it is possible to turn the long call into a call ratio spread.

5

Call Writing

By the end of this chapter you should be able to:

- ▲ Understand the mechanics of option writing.

- ▲ Develop a strategy using scrip-covered call writing and the different types of covered writes.

- ▲ Use naked call option writing as a strategy.

- ▲ Evaluate possible positions based on their degree of aggressiveness.

- ▲ Recognise situations requiring defensive action.

- ▲ Calculate margin payment requirements.

Option Writing

It is the concept of option writing that almost always causes inexperienced options traders difficulty. The easiest way to understand this is as a variation of short selling; we are merely selling something (an option) in the hope that either:

- ▲ we will be able to buy it back at a cheaper price, realising a profit;

- ▲ it will expire worthless for which we also receive a profit; or

- ▲ it will be exercised and we will earn a capital gain.

In terms of the Australian market, call writing falls naturally into two types: scrip-covered call writing and naked call writing, which is often referred to as 'cash' or collateral covered. Scrip-covered writing refers to a situation were there is underlying stock ownership and, conversely, going naked means there is no stock ownership involved.

Scrip-covered Call Writing

There are two principal reasons why traders write options against stock they hold: firstly, to provide downside protection, and secondly, to increase the rate of return of the stock they hold. These two factors are inextricably linked; option writing for downside protection will increase the rate of return. Likewise, option writing to increase the rate of return will also offer downside protection. However, do not overestimate the roll of option writing in providing downside protection—the best downside protection is to use a stop loss. It's cheap and effective.

Before looking at an example of option writing it is necessary to consider the limitations of this strategy. Much is made of the notion of buying shares on margin and then immediately writing options quite close to the money to generate cash to pay the interest cost. This is based on a misunderstanding of the level of return that can be generated by such a strategy and the costs associated with exercise. It is also contradictory in its view of the market.

For example, if I borrow money to buy shares, I am by definition bullish. If I buy a call option then I am neutral to bearish. To execute both trades simultaneously defeats the purpose of margin lending.

In my opinion covered writing is only of use when you have a share that is in a long-term uptrend as defined by a weekly chart. During a long-term move there will be shorter-term countertrend moves. These shorter-term moves may provide an opportunity to write options.

It needs to be remembered that margin lending is a wealth creation tool, so as long as our shares are in an uptrend we want to hang on to them. As a consequence of this, should the underlying start to rise and the written call be threatened, we will have to take some defensive action to preserve the integrity of the underlying position.

As an example of this, let's assume we hold 3,000 ANZ shares which were purchased for $18.00. In conjunction with holding these shares, we sell three ANZ July 1950 calls for 50¢. By doing this we have established a scrip-covered write.

From the sale of our option, we will receive $1,500 (representing the option premium, i.e. $3 \times 1,000 \times 50¢$); if ANZ finishes below $19.50 in October the call will expire worthless and we pocket the $1,500. Simultaneously, we have established $1,500 worth of downside protection—that is, we can have ANZ drop by 50¢ before we enter our theoretical loss zone. It must be stressed that implicit in this example was the assumption that we had purchased ANZ for $18.00 and hence we defined our theoretical loss zone as being $18.00 minus 50¢ —that is, our stock entry price minus the option premium received. In reality, traders will have to input their own entry price into the equation. As a simple rule, never write options with strike prices below your entry price—you should have used your stop loss long before you reached this point.

If we had purchased ANZ for $18.00 and immediately written an option against it, we would have performed what is known as a 'buy and write strategy'. However, remember this is performing two conflicting strategies.

Taking our example from above, let's examine what happens should ANZ rise in price. If ANZ rises moderately in price, we may enjoy the best of both worlds. Should ANZ finish at or just below $19.50 then our option will expire worthless, and we will have the benefit of a slight rise in the price of our shares on top of the premium for the options.

If ANZ rallies strongly, then we have a variety of alternatives. As with all options strategies, the alternative exists to do nothing. In such an instance, if ANZ had risen well above $19.50 and our option was then in-the-money, then our option would be exercised and our stock called away. However, in doing nothing we lose the prime driver of our wealth creation strategy.

Our profit from such an occurrence would then comprise our initial premium of $1,500 (50¢ per share) plus the profit from the sale of our shares at $19.50. Whilst we would have made a profit on the transaction we would no longer own the shares, which are now well above the $19.50 we just sold them for. This represents an opportunity cost that should not be underestimated.

This brings us to a very important consideration; you must only write options against shares you are willing to sell.

Instead of having our stock called away, we have a second alternative. Suppose ANZ has risen to $21.30. Our 1950 option will then be selling for its intrinsic value of $1.80. If we covered or bought back the option we would lose 1.30¢ per share (or $3,900 on our three contracts), having sold the calls originally for 30¢. However, we have removed our obligation to sell our shares at $19.50. So in reality whilst it has cost us $3,900 to buy our option back, we have an unrealised gain of $3.30 on each share as defined by the current sale price minus original purchase price, i.e. $21.30 – $18.00 = $3.30 unrealised profit. The astute reader will have realised that by closing out our option at $19.50 we are now free to write an option at a higher strike price should the opportunity arise—thereby increasing our potential profit. Such a tactic is known as rolling up.

We have the opportunity to buy back the option, a course of action we should take the moment we realise the trade has gone wrong. The flexibility of options allows us to undertake a variety of repair strategies. For example, to remove the obligation of the 1950 written call we could simply purchase a 1900 call. In doing so we would have constructed a call bull spread. Such an action is only restorative in nature—it doesn't allow us the chance to profit dramatically from a runaway move.

To profit from a runaway move we can do something a little more complex. We can convert our written position into what is known as a call ratio backspread by purchasing two calls at

2000. The addition of the two higher strike priced calls converts the bearish written call to a bullish trade. The sequence of events is:

1. Buy shares at $18.00.

2. Sell 1950 call.

3. Share price rises. As a result we are in danger of losing our stock. As a result we implement repair strategies.

4. We can implement the following:

    ▶   Set a hard money stop and simply buy the option back. The loss incurred is offset by the unrealised gain in the share.

    ▶   Convert the trade into a spread by purchasing a lower strike price call.

    ▶   Turn the position into a call ratio backspread by purchasing two higher strike price calls. This converts a neutral/bearish trade into an outright directional trade. In an ideal situation the stock would continue to rise and the backspread would be profitable. The shares would be retained and the backspread closed at a profit.

What Options to Write

Traders who engage in option writing are faced with the decision as to what options to write. Often new traders are seduced by the prospect of writing long-dated close to the money options. It is thought that the large premiums offered by such options will insulate the trader against an adverse move. However, think back to our earlier discussion on option buying. We concluded that we should only buy options with the following characteristics:

1. Enough time to expiry to insulate us as much as possible from the effects of time decay (generally not less than 45 days). This also means a higher vega.

2. Relatively high gamma. This means our bought options will be at-the-money where gamma is highest.

3. If you have a volatility component to your trading then you would seek to buy options that are undervalued.

For the sake of simplicity we can assume that the rules for writing options are the reverse of those for buying, so:

1. Write options with little time to expiry, preferably less than 45 days to go. This way the decay is working for us. The low time to expiry will insulate against spikes in volatility.

2. Sell options with low gamma. Such options are by definition out-of-the-money.

3. Preferably sell options that are overvalued with regard to their implied volatility.

If our trading has a technical component to it, such as trying to catch breakouts or trend reversals, then we will also need some general rules for option writing:

1. Understand the current major trend of the underlying. Written positions are for stagnant or gently upwardly trending stocks. This may seem obvious but few traders actually understand trends and consistently trade against them.

2. Look for a logical zone of resistance and then write above this.

3. Calculate the standard deviation for a share using the same time period as the option expiry you want to write and use it to plot a zone for writing.

Before moving on to look at naked writing I need to issue a warning: if you engage in naked option writing you are exposing yourself to potentially unlimited losses. If you do not understand this and/or you do not institute a risk management program which revolves around the most basic of survival skills (the stop loss) *do not under any circumstances consider naked option writing.*

The Mechanics of Option Writing

Having described the fundamental theory behind scrip-covered option writing, it is necessary that the trader be aware of the procedural requirements of option writing.

If you are writing options against stock you already own, then it is necessary to lodge your scrip with the Options Clearing House (OCH). Along with this, you lodge a bulk scrip depository receipt and standard transfer. Although it is unlikely (because of carrying costs) that your option will be exercised early, it is possible and you must be ready for it. Exercise and assignment happen automatically; the first you will know about it is when your broker receives an exercise notice from the OCH and from this point the events cannot be altered. It should also be stressed that exercise is totally random—it cannot be predicted nor can it be reversed.

Whilst your scrip is held by the OCH you remain at all times its owner. All benefits of stock ownership accrue to you: all dividends, bonuses or other issues remain yours.

Naked Call Option Writing

If a trader writes/sells a call option without owning the underlying stock, then this person is said to have written a 'naked option'. Naked option writing has a limited potential profit and, theoretically, *unlimited potential loss.*

To illustrate this relationship assume we have written WMC Sept 900 calls for 50¢. Our maximum profit potential is limited to 50¢—the premium we have received. Yet our potential for loss is unlimited. If WMC rallies strongly, then we risk having to buy back our option at greater than parity or being exercised. Remember that by writing a call option we have obligated ourselves to deliver a given number of shares at a certain price if required to do so. Given that we have written our option at the $9.00 strike price, if WMC finishes above $9.50, our breakeven, we will be in a loss situation. A range of possible outcomes is shown below. (Remember, our breakeven point is determined by adding the premium to our strike price.)

Note how our profit is limited to our initial credit; yet once we reach our breakeven point our loss is unlimited if we were to attempt to buy our position back (as shown in Figure 5.1).

Figure 5.1 *WMC Written Call (Naked)*

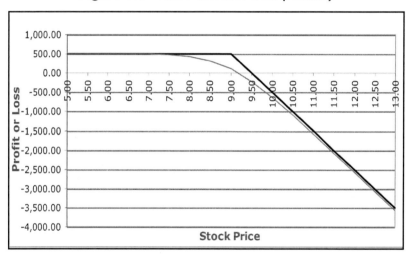

A naked option writer will not necessarily lose money if the stock moves up—a loss will only be incurred if the underlying share finishes above the breakeven point. Remember from our earlier discussion on pricing that a fall in volatility may cause the price of an option to fall. Likewise time decay will be acting upon the option as the underlying moves. Clearly, even though potentially the loss is theoretically unlimited, in reality this is not so since a stock cannot rise to infinity. However, this small realisation does not offset the pain of a runaway position. It is worth remembering that options values can inflate very quickly, so a form of harm minimisation is essential.

Degree of Aggressiveness

The risk/reward criteria for this strategy are dependent upon the aggressiveness of the trader. Very aggressive traders would often consider writing an in-the-money call, thereby granting themselves a larger potential profit but with accompanying higher risk. The writing of an in-the-money option is very aggressive and is often considered analogous to being short a futures contract. Only those with a precise understanding of option pricing, volatility trading, risk management and repair strategies should contemplate such trades. Conversely, the writer of an out-of-the-money call will achieve a smaller return but with relatively less risk.

Defensive Action

As previously stated, if our underlying stock rises above our breakeven point, then we lose money either by having to buy our option back or by being exercised and having to deliver stock. However, this can be avoided by using a carefully designed fall-back action. Firstly, the breakeven point needs to be carefully defined. Once this point is reached, we have to decide if we should quit the stock permanently.

It is essential that losses be culled immediately. To not do so is to invite disaster. It should be noted that if you have written a naked call then you are on the wrong side of an uptrend. Such a situation should not be allowed to persist.

It cannot be stressed strongly enough that the first line of defence that a trader has is a stop loss. When your trade has gone wrong you should leave ASAP.

The easiest way to define a stop loss is simply to decide how much money you are willing to lose before a position is closed. Unfortunately for most traders who engage in option writing this decision comes too late and they donate a large amount of money to the market.

Understanding Margin Requirements

It is important for traders in the options market to understand that their obligations when trading options are often markedly different from when trading shares. The most apparent of these differences becomes obvious when options are written. Throughout this book reference has been made to strategies where either naked or covered options are written. Undertaking these strategies brings certain obligations, including the possibility of having to make margin payments. Because of the confusion that often surrounds these situations it is necessary to review your obligations before moving on to a discussion of how the margining system operates.

The seller of a call undertakes to sell to the call buyer the underlying share at a fixed price on or before the expiry date. In this situation, if the call buyer decides to call away the stock from you, you have to supply that stock at the price specified in the options contract. For example, if you have sold an ANZ July 2000 call and that call is exercised by the buyer, you have to supply ANZ at $20.00, irrespective of the current market price. Such a situation presents you with limited risk if you own the underlying share. The only risk you face is the opportunity cost of having your BHP-Billiton called away in what may be a rising market.

If you are, however, a naked option writer then you are faced with a very serious dilemma. Using the same example consider that you have written an ANZ July 2000 call but you have done so without owning any ANZ shares. Consider that ANZ has risen to $23.00 and the call you have written is exercised. Then you have to sell to the call buyer ANZ at $20.00, despite the fact that ANZ is trading in the market for $23.00. So you have to buy ANZ at $23.00 and sell it for $20.00, a loss of $3.00 (plus brokerage per share). If you had sold ten contracts then you would be looking at a loss of in excess of $30,000. Once you have received your exercise notice there is nothing you can do about it; default is not a possibility.

A set of analogous responsibilities applies to the sellers or writers of put options. In writing a put you have obligated yourself to take delivery of the underlying share at the price specified by the option strike price. For example, if you had sold an ANZ July 2000 put, then you have guaranteed that you will, if required, take delivery of ANZ at $20.00 per share irrespective of the market price. If you assume that ANZ has fallen to $17.00 and your contract is exercised then you are required to take delivery of ANZ at $20.00. If you are not in a financial position to hold ANZ then you will have to on-sell ANZ to the market. In doing so, you are crystallising a loss of approximately $3.00 per share. If you had written ten contracts then you would be looking at a loss of $30,000 if you were not in a position to hold indefinitely $200,000 worth of ANZ.

Many new entrants to the options market are often confused and irritated by the need for margin payments when writing options. If you have been one of those who is irritated by margins, consider either of the above examples and whether you could survive the financial strain imposed upon you by such a situation.

Margins are used for many reasons. They protect the financial viability of the options market by guaranteeing that any obligations you might have are met. They protect your broker from your possible default in a situation where the financial burden of a trade becomes too great. Finally, and most importantly, they protect you by giving an exact idea of the status of your trade. Nothing focuses the mind like repeated margin calls. Consider how the system would work if, instead of progressive margining, you were faced with the need to make a single lump-sum payment at the termination of a position. Such a system would be prone to default as traders, unaware of their obligations throughout the life of the trade, collapsed under the weight of a single payment.

How to Calculate Margins

At first glance the margining system that the OCH uses—which goes by the name Theoretical Intermarket Margining System (TIMS)—appears rather complicated. However, like everything to do with options it becomes much simpler when it is broken down into its component parts.

Scrip-covered Options

In the situation of a buy and write, an options trader sells options against stock already owned. For example, if you owned 5,000 WMC and sold five WMC calls against this stock position you would have established a scrip-covered write. The shares you own are lodged with the OCH and they serve as collateral for this strategy. As such you incur no further margin obligations. If you are exercised you simply fulfil your obligation by selling the underlying shares.

There is a second method whereby someone who owns shares not involved in the options trade may use those shares as collateral for the purposes of writing options. The OCH will assign a collateral value to shares that have been lodged as security. This system works in the following manner:

The OCH has established three tiers of shares that are acceptable to be lodged as security.

Tier One in the jargon of the OCH refers to securities approved as underlying securities under Rule 7.4.1 and securities which fit the criteria for approval under that Rule but which are not currently approved. In simple terms any share that has exchange-traded options may be lodged as collateral. For example, you could lodge ANZ shares for the purposes of writing TLS options.

Tier Two is any share or units in entities within the ASX50 which do not fall within the shares listed in Tier One.

Tier Three is any exchange-traded security of Tier One shares, other than fully paid ordinary shares that meet the following criteria: issued capital represented by the securities must be a minimum of $100 million; the minimum monthly volume must be in excess of 100,000 units; and the minimum closing price must be at least 50¢.

In defining how much the collateral you have lodged is worth, the OCH applies a discount to the market value of your shares. The purpose of applying a discount is to guard against a sudden change in the market value of your shares. Such a treatment provides both you and the OCH with a buffer against unexpected market volatility. At the time of writing this discount is 30% of the total market value of the shares you have lodged.

For example, if we assume you have lodged 5,000 ANZ shares with a market value of $18.00, the market value of your basket of shares is $90,000. In applying a collateral value to these shares the OCH subtracts 30% of the market value of the shares, so the value of your collateral is $90,000 − 30% = $63,000. You therefore have $63,000 available to fulfil your margin obligations.

Collateral must be lodged with the OCH by 4 p.m. of the day in which the trade is initiated. So if you put a trade into the market in the morning you must lodge your collateral by 4 p.m. of the same day. If you do not do this the OCH will treat your position as uncovered and full margins will be payable in cash by 11 a.m. of the following morning.

As well as taking shares as security the OCH will accept a range of other financial instruments such as bank guarantees, certificates of deposit and non-bank bills of exchange.

Calculating Margins for Exchange-Traded Options

The total margin payable by traders when they have written a naked position is made up of two components, the premium margin and risk margin.

The premium margin represents the current price you would get for your option if it were liquidated at the end of the day.

Risk margin, which is also known as the initial margin, is the amount that represents the largest likely daily move in the value of the option. The calculation of this variation is based upon historical models of the price movements and current market volatility of the underlying share.

Calculating Premium Margins

Let's assume you have written an ANZ Oct 1850 call for $1.13. The premium margin would simply be the premium you received, $1,130.00. Remember the terms price and premium are interchangeable, so if you are having difficulty working out your premium risk just think of it as being a deposit that is equivalent to the price of your option. The situation is similar for the buyers of options but in this case the premium paid is treated as a credit, not a debit as in the case of written options. You might ask what relevance is an example of the situation with bought options. Bought options play a role in determining margins.

If, for example, you use our original case of having sold an ANZ Oct 1850 call for $1.13 you would be liable for a margin of $1,130.00. However, if in conjunction with the short in ANZ you had also bought a St George Sept 2232 call for 90¢ (or $900) then you would be eligible for what is termed an 'offset'.

The practice of offsets allows portfolios of options to be matched against one another. Such a practice recognises the reality that a market cannot simultaneously go both up and down, therefore as one position loses value another gains value.

The offset in our example would work in the following way:

Short 1 ANZ Oct 1850 call @ $1.13 = $1,130.00 debit margin

Long 1 St George Sept 2232 call @ $0.90 = $ 900.00 credit margin

The total margin position is calculated by subtracting the credit margin from the debit margin. In this example there is a total premium margin payable of $230. The OCH, in calculating the total premium margin, seeks to take into consideration the net margin position of all open positions across all option classes for that account. Calculating your premium margin is simply a matter of summing up all your premiums.

We can further illustrate this by extending our example and adding two more positions:

Short 1 ANZ Oct 1850 call @ $1.13 = $1,130.00 debit margin

Long 1 St George Sept 2232 call @ $0.90 = $ 900.00 credit margin

Short 1 AMP Sept 1850 put @ 73¢ = $730 debit margin

Long 1 WMC Dec 750 put @ 17¢ = $170 credit margin

A bit of simple arithmetic gives us our total premium margin position, i.e. $1,130 − $900 + $730 − $170 = $790 debit margin. Note that this is a debit because the dollar value of our short trades exceeds that of our long trades. There is also no difference in the treatment of short puts and calls versus long puts and calls; any short or written position can offset any long or bought position.

Calculating Risk Margins

Risk margin is defined by the OCH as being the largest probable daily move in the value of an option based upon a study of the historical movement in price and the current market volatilities of the underlying security. In other words, the OCH looks at how volatile a share has been for a period of six months. This gives a guide to the possible range of movement that a share may move in during a period of normal market activity. This study of a share's volatility generates a figure known as the 'margin interval', which is expressed as a percentage of the share's value.

If a share such as WMC has a current market value of $7.30 and its margin interval has been calculated to be 8%—which is equivalent to 58¢ either side of the current market price—then based upon the margin interval the stock is unlikely to either fall below $6.72 or rise above $7.88 the next trading day. In essence we have established a theoretical range based upon a review of historical data within which our stock may move.

However, such information on its own is largely useless in defining our margin commitments. In order to determine how this may affect our margin commitment it is necessary to understand how a move in the underlying share will affect our option. To do this it is necessary to review the concept of delta. As defined earlier in this book, delta is the amount an option will move given a specific rise in the underlying stock. If an option had a delta of 1.0 then for every 1¢ move in the underlying share the option would also move 1¢. Conversely if an option had a delta of 0.5 then the underlying share would have to move 2¢ for the option to move 1¢.

To take our WMC example our margin interval is 8% or 58¢ based upon the current market value of $7.30. Let's assume that we have sold the WMC Oct 775 call for 30¢ and that this option has a delta of 0.26.

To calculate our risk margin we have to recalculate the value of our option, taking into account the range of possible prices as defined by our margin interval. So our risk margin is calculated by multiplying our maximum rise in price by the delta of our option:

58¢ x 0.26 = 15¢

Our total margin commitment is our premium margin (current market price) plus our risk margin:

30¢ + 15¢ = 45¢ or $450.00 per contract

It should be noted that we only have to revalue our option on the upside since we are only interested in the maximum possible move against our position. A fall in WMC would add value to our position.

In calculating your margin requirements the OCH uses the binomial model outlined in Chapter 2 and what is termed 'modern portfolio theory'.

When actual margins are levied against your account you are going to have to trust that the figures supplied to you by the OCH and your broker are correct. To calculate all the margins required by your account, particularly if you are trading a basket of options, is largely a waste of your time and effort and requires a mathematical competency that is beyond most traders. If you have difficulty in accepting the figures you are given all I can say is that in all my time dealing in options I have never seen an error in a margin statement. If you baulk at the level of margins required to be paid then you don't fully understand that margins are there for everyone's protection.

If all this seems somewhat perplexing the ASX has a margin calculator available on its website.

Traders who complain about margins often remind me of the old story of the customer in the Porsche dealership who was worried about fuel economy; if you can't afford the petrol you can't afford the car. The same is true for margins; if you can't afford them then you should not be trading this particular side of the market.

Figure 5.2 *Call Writing Selection Summary*

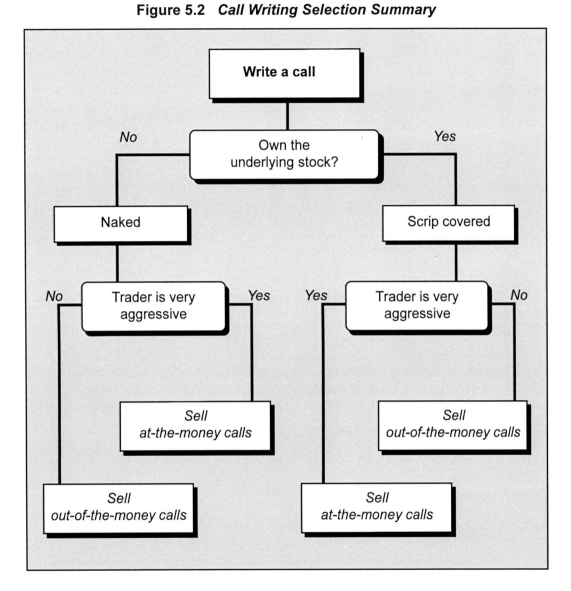

Call Writing Summary

Time Decay: Helps.

Volatility: Hurts.

Potential Profit: Limited to the premium received.

Potential loss: Theoretically unlimited

Sensitivity Analysis

Delta: Delta will approach 1.0 as the position moves to being in-the-money.

Gamma: When we are short calls we are carrying what are known as short or negative gamma positions.

Theta: Time decay assists short call positions.

Vega: Volatility is the enemy of the short trader. The relationship between volatility and an option's price is linear.

What Can Go Wrong

▶ *Poor market analysis.* It is essential to trade in the direction of the trend. Writing a call is dependent upon either a slack market or one that drifts downwards. If you are extremely bearish it is often better to generate a put-based strategy rather than sell a call.

▶ *Poor call selection.* Traders often have poor call selection.

▶ *Too much time.* Time decay is the ally of the written call.

If It Does Go Wrong

▶ Practice strong money management. Have a defined stop loss point that you will exit at.

▶ It is possible to repair some short call positions. For example, if the market is moving upwards you have a few alternatives, the wisest of which in most cases is simply to leave. However if you are naked the call then you may buy the underlying stock to fulfil your obligation. The same result can be achieved by buying a call with a lower strike price and turning the strategy into a spread. A more advanced repair can be used if your view switches from neutral/bearish to very bullish, and that is to create a call ratio backspread—keep the call you have written and buy two calls with higher strike prices.

6

Put Buying

By the end of this chapter you should be able to:

▲ Select appropriate put options to buy depending on your outlook.

▲ Understand how a put strategy can offer downside protection.

▲ Realise that puts have different time value characteristics to calls.

▲ Develop a strategy to take defensive action.

A Tool for Bearish Investors

Just as call buying is a bullish strategy, put buying is a bearish strategy and can be a very effective tool in a falling market. A put option buyer is convinced there will be a downward movement in the stock during the life of the option.

In many instances the concepts outlined in Chapter 4 may be reversed and applied to puts with equal efficiency.

An initial difference put buyers must come to terms with is the concept of in-the-money and out-of-the-money. In reference to call options an option which has a strike price lower than the stock's current price is said to be in-the-money. An option with a strike price which is higher than the stock price is out-of-the-money. The situation is reversed with put options. A put option is considered to be in-the-money when the strike price of the option is higher than that of the stock.

Put options do not trade in the same volume as call options, yet traders buy them for many of the same reasons that they buy call options. In practice, there are two prime reasons.

Leverage

Put option buying is a leveraged alternative to short selling stock. In short selling a stock, a trader sells a stock he or she does not own in the hope of buying it back at a cheaper price, thereby profiting from a fall in the price. This is a very risky strategy should the stock rise sharply. By buying put options, for a small cash outlay, a trader can profit substantially from a fall in a stock price, at limited risk. A short seller's risk is, theoretically, unlimited.

Downside Protection

The purchase of a put can be used to limit the downside in stock that is already owned. When a trader owns stock and a put covering that same stock, then there is limited downside during the life of the put.

For example, if we purchase AMP at $17.75 and we simultaneously purchase an AMP July 1750 put at 30¢, the put gives us the right to sell our stock at $17.50. Therefore the maximum we can lose on our stock is $17.75 – $17.50 = 25¢ (see Figure 6.1). Since we have paid 30¢ for our put, our maximum potential loss during the life of our put is 55¢. However, if the stock goes up we stand a chance of losing our investment in the put. This is compensated for by unrealised gains on our stock.

Figure 6.1   *AMP Downside Protection*

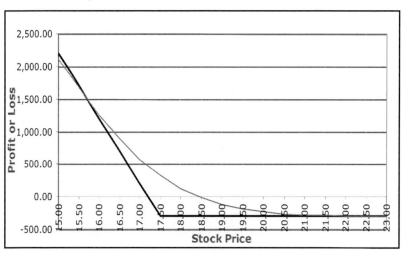

Thus, our put purchase has acted like an insurance policy with a limited life.

In general, there are two types of traders who may opt for this approach. The first is the long-term trader who wants some protection during the life of the put. As a long-term holder, it is unlikely that such a trader will actually sell stock via exercise. The purchase of a low-cost put will aid in rectifying some of the damage done to a portfolio by sudden drops in price.

The second type of traders are those who are taking a position in a stock and may also consider the purchase of a put. This will aid in offsetting any losses if they have entered the stock at the wrong time. It is possible to simultaneously buy the stock and the put.

However the cost of this insurance needs to be considered. Hedging is an expensive undertaking and has limited utility because of this. It should be remembered that if I buy a share for $10 and then buy a long-dated put for $1 the purchase price of my stock is $11. I now have to show a 20% gain on the stock to breakeven.

A much cheaper strategy is simply to use a stop loss—stops are free and can be initiated electronically.

How to Select a Put

This has been adequately covered in Chapter 4. Although the discussion there was focused on call options, it applies similarly to selecting stocks for writing puts.

Which Put?

The same generic rules that guided our selection of call options also guide our put selection:

1. We want to achieve maximum bang for bucks so we will go for options with the highest gamma.

2. In being long puts we are also long vega (volatility). Changes in volatility are highest in options with longer expiries and at-the-money strike prices.

3. Time decay is the enemy of the option buyer so we need to buy time. The purchase of short-dated out-of-the-money options is extremely dangerous.

Timing

The general rules on timing covered in Chapter 4 also apply to puts. However, a few points are worth noting. Put options have slightly different time decay characteristics. With call options it is only possible to buy substantial time value at a higher premium. With put options, it is not unusual to see very little time value even in long-dated options.

It is not unusual to see the sort of situation shown in Table 6.1.

Table 6.1 *Time Value in Calls and Puts*

BHP trading @ $10.00

Call Options	Price	Put Options	Price
May 1000	65¢	May 475	50¢
Aug 1000	110¢	Aug 475	95¢
Nov 1000	145¢	Nov 475	130¢

Notice how there is substantially more time value in the calls versus the puts. (This is also demonstrated in Figure 2.4.) This affects the timing of our decision in the following way.

If we can purchase extra time for a relatively small increase in the premium, then we can effectively hedge our timing at very little cost. We are able to buy time cheaply, hence we add in a margin for error.

Stock Volatility

The text in Chapter 4 covers stock volatility for both puts and calls. Rather than repeat the information, I suggest you refer back to this if you need a refresher.

Defensive Action

Just as a broad range of tactics were available to the call buyer, so too are they available to put option buyers. However, your first tactic should always be a simple stop loss.

Locking-in Profits

Once again, if we are presented with a potential profit we can opt for one of four possible alternatives.

Firstly, the position could be closed and we would pocket our profit and retire. Such a strategy removes all risk, but it also removes any further profit potential. Once again, this is a non-aggressive strategy.

Secondly, we could elect to do nothing—as stated before, this tactic shouldn't even be considered as it is very risky to turn your back in a dynamic market.

Thirdly, we may, in effect, roll down our investment by selling our initial put option, recouping our original costs and investing the rest in a lower priced put. This allows us to retain our original investment, thereby reducing the risk of capital loss while allowing us to maintain a position in the stock, and possibly enhance our profit potential. In this strategy we are allowing the trend to be our friend.

Finally, we may create a spread by selling an out-of-the-money put against our original long position. In such a situation, we can still profit from any further downward movement in the stock and if it reverses direction, our short position will decrease in value and insulate us from any severe price rise in the underlying stock. Once again, this alternative also lends itself to rectifying a losing position since the premium income from the short position would help offset any unrealised loss. Naturally, this strategy works best if the underlying stock stabilises in price.

Figure 6.2 *Put Buying Selection Summary*

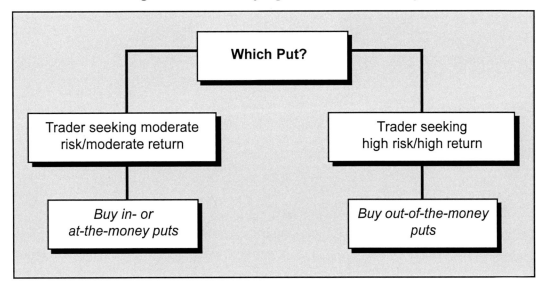

Put Buying Summary

Time Decay: Hurts.

Volatility: Helps.

Potential profit: Profit can be unlimited in a falling market.

Potential loss: Limited to the premium that was paid. This aspect makes this a good strategy for those who are new to debit trades to practise on.

Sensitivity Analysis

Delta: Moves towards 1.0 as the option moves into the money.

Gamma: Gamma falls rapidly as we move into-the-money or out-of-the-money.

Theta: Time decay will kill this position. Theta will accelerate throughout the life of the trade.

Vega: A long put is a long volatility trade. It is aided by an increase in volatility. Vega will increase as the underlying moves towards the strike price.

What Can Go Wrong

▶ *Poor market analysis.* It is essential to trade in the direction of the trend. Put buying is a strategy designed for strong moves.

▶ *Poor put selection.* Traders often have poor put selection.

▶ *Not enough time.* Time decay is the enemy of the put.

If It Does Go Wrong

▶ Practise strong money management. Have a defined stop loss point that you will exit at.

▶ It is possible to repair some long put positions. For example, if the market stalls and your perspective goes from strongly bearish to moderately bearish you could turn the position into a bear put spread by selling a put with a lower strike price. If your view goes from bearish to bullish it is possible to turn the long put into a put ratio spread.

Put Writing

By the end of this chapter you should be able to:

- Develop an appropriate strategy for naked put writing.
- Take defensive action to limit potential losses.
- Use writing puts as a strategy to acquire stock at below market prices.

Writing Puts versus Buying Puts

In buying a put, a trader has paid a premium for the right but not the obligation to sell stock at a given price some time in the future. Hence, the writer of a put is obligated to buy that stock at the given strike price.

The easiest way to remember this is to realise that a put option writer will have stock put to him or her if the strategy goes wrong.

Traders may write puts for two general reasons: the first is merely to speculate on a rising market. The second is a way to try and buy stock at below market prices.

Naked Put Writing

At this point it is worth noting that writing puts differs from writing calls as all put writing is 'naked'. There is no such thing as 'covered' put writing. This is because you are selling someone the right to sell a share (as opposed to the right to buy it) so whether you actually own the stock is of no consequence—on exercise no-one will be trying to buy it from you.

Speculation

Put writing is inherently bullish and theoretically has *unlimited loss potential*. Let's take a look at an example.

Assume we are bullish on NCP and seek to take advantage of any upward swing in the stock price. NCP is trading at $10.00 and we decide that the stock should advance from this price. So we sell or write an NCP August 950 put for which we receive 50¢. This 50¢ represents our maximum profit potential (realised if these options expire worthless) yet our loss can be theoretically unlimited.

The possible range of outcomes is shown in Figure 7.1.

Figure 7.1 *NCP Written Put*

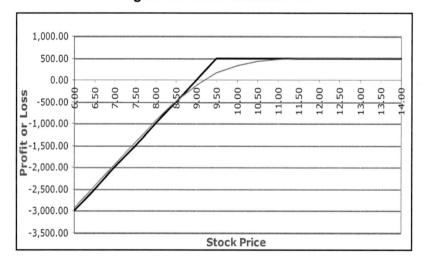

Note how our profit is limited to our initial premium but our loss is potentially unlimited. In this situation, it is assumed that the option was bought back before expiry, thereby eliminating the possibility of being exercised.

It should be noted that being exercised will also result in a greater loss than buying the option back. Such an anomaly results from brokerage and stamp duty costs, and the potential inability for traders to sell stock that has been put to them at an adequate price. Put writers will be exercised if the market falls heavily. This will result in them paying over-the-market prices for stock and then attempting to on-sell this stock into a falling market.

How aggressive traders wish to be will determine which put they write. The least aggressive option is to write an out-of-the-money put; that is, write a put with a strike price below the current market price of the stock.

A very aggressive put writer may seek to write a deeply in-the-money put for which he or she will receive a larger premium.

Defensive Action

As with call writing, the put option writer must have a fall-back plan if the situation goes awry.

The simplest of actions is merely to buy back the position and take the resultant loss. Often this is possible without incurring too great a loss since a put option will lose its time value very quickly once it is in-the-money. In closing out a position immediately we recognise the potential for a loss, and we dramatically limit the size of the loss. In doing so we admit that we are on the wrong side of the trend, thereby freeing ourselves to take advantage of the underlying trend instead of attempting to trade against it. Hoping and hanging on is not a strategy that will promote long-term survival.

Writing Puts to Acquire Stock

Some traders take the innovative step of writing puts against stock they wish to acquire below current market price. This approach is appropriate for a sideways market that is merely drifting. Such a market offers the chance for the trader to be exercised without the market swinging too far away from the entry point.

Imagine we are wishing to take a position in ANZ which is currently trading at $18.50; however, we consider it to be a better buy at $18.00 or below. So we write an ANZ July 1850 put for which we receive 75¢. If ANZ is below $18.00 at expiry, there is a good probability that we will have the stock put to us at $18.50. If such a situation occurred, we would have bought ANZ for $17.75, representing the option strike price minus the premium we have received. Therefore, if ANZ is within the range of $17.75 to $18.50 at expiry, we will have effectively bought it at below market price.

If ANZ is above $18.50 at expiry, we merely pocket the premium we have received and try again. The downside to such a technique is that if ANZ falls substantially, say to $17.00, we would still be paying an effective $17.75 per share.

A Quick Quiz

Put option writing is considered to be a relatively risky strategy due to the risk/reward character of the payoff profile. Conversely, covered call writing is considered to be a relatively safe strategy. However, examine the following payoff diagrams. Which represents a covered call and which represents a written put? The answer is below.

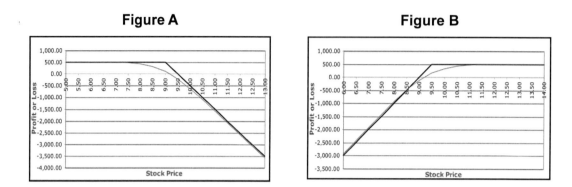

Figure A   **Figure B**

Both the written put and the covered call are represented by the same payoff diagram (Figure B). They are in essence identical. A good way to test the knowledge of many self-proclaimed option gurus is to ask them which is riskier—a covered call or a written put.

Figure 7.2 *Put Writing Selection Summary*

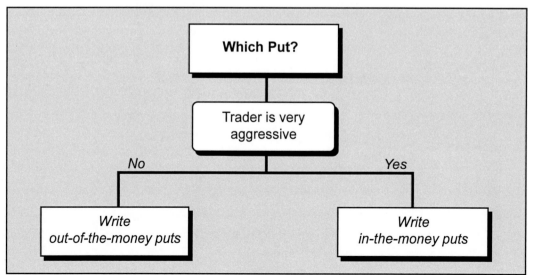

Put Writing Summary

Time Decay: Helps.

Volatility: Hurts.

Potential profit: Limited to the premium received.

Potential loss: Theoretically unlimited.

Sensitivity Analysis

Delta: Delta will approach 1.0 as the position moves to being in-the-money.

Gamma: When we are short puts we are carrying what are known as short or negative gamma positions.

Theta: Time decay assists short put positions.

Vega: Volatility is the enemy of the short trader. The relationship between volatility and an option's price is linear. If volatility goes up then the value of the option goes up.

What Can Go Wrong

▶ *Poor market analysis.* It is essential to trade in the direction of the trend. Writing a put is dependent upon either a slack market or one that drifts upwards. If you are extremely bullish it is often better to generate a call-based strategy rather than sell a put.

▶ *Poor put selection.* As has been mentioned traders often have poor put selection.

If It Does Go Wrong

▶ Practise strong money management. Have a defined stop loss point that you will exit at.

▶ It is possible to repair some short put positions. For example, if the market is moving upwards you have a few alternatives, the wisest of which usually is simply to leave. You can also buy a put with a higher strike price and turn the strategy into a spread. A more advanced repair can be used if your view switches from neutral/bullish to very bearish, and that is to create a put ratio backspread—keep the put you have written and buy two puts with lower strike prices.

8

Spreads, Straddles and Strangles

<u>A spread is created</u> with the simultaneous buying and selling of options of the same underlying security but with differing strike prices. Spreads are amongst the most popular strategies available to options traders. Spreads can be either bullish or bearish in their outlook; likewise they may be created by using either calls or puts. Hence, we can have call and put bull spreads and call and put bear spreads.

Bull Spreads

Call Bull Spreads

A call bull spread is created by buying a low strike price call and selling a higher strike price call. Assume the following option prices:

> BHP is trading at $10.50
>
> BHP Oct 1050 call is trading at 55¢
>
> BHP Oct 1100 call is trading at 30¢

If we were to buy the BHP Oct 1050 call at 55¢ and sell the BHP 1100 Oct call at 30¢, we would have created a bull spread. Note that this is a debit transaction—it costs us money to set up. Any spread that costs money to initiate is a debit spread.

A bull spread is profitable if the stock moves up in price. This spread has limited profit potential and limited risk.

Figure 8.1 shows a range of possible outcomes.

Figure 8.1   *Call Bull Spread Payoff Diagram*

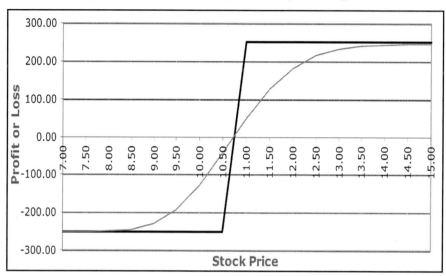

Two points are evident:

1.   Our maximum profit is realised if the stock finishes at or above the higher strike price.

2.   A maximum loss is incurred if the stock is at or below the lower strike price.

As with all strategies, a breakeven point can be easily defined.

In this instance, breakeven is the lower strike price plus the net debit of the spread. Hence, breakeven is: 1050 + 25 = 1075¢

You may already have realised that this is not an overwhelmingly bullish play since we have limited our risk, at the expense of our maximum potential profit. A trader who was very aggressive would purchase the lower strike price by itself, and naturally such a strategy would outperform the bull spread if the stock moved up sharply.

Put Bull Spreads

A put bull spread is established by buying a put at a lower strike price and selling a put at a higher strike price. Note that this is exactly the same way we established a call bull spread.

To illustrate the construction of such a spread, consider the following prices:

BHP is trading at $10.50

BHP June 950 put is trading at 50¢

BHP June 1000 put is trading at 70¢

If we buy the June 950 put and sell the June 1000 put, we have again created a bull spread. Unlike the call bull spread this is a credit transaction. Such spreads are referred to as credit spreads. In this example the credit is 20¢. Figure 8.2 shows possible outcomes.

Figure 8.2   *Put Bull Spread Payoff Diagram*

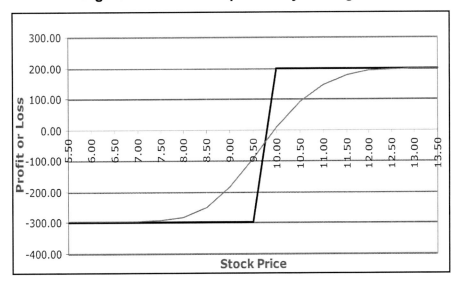

In this instance, our maximum profit is restricted to our initial credit of 20¢ and the maximum loss occurs if our stock is at or below our lower strike price at expiry.

The breakeven point of this type of strategy is equal to the higher strike price minus net credit. Thus, in this example, our breakeven is: 1000 – 20 = 980¢.

In general, call bull spreads are superior to put bull spreads. The major disadvantage with put bull spreads is that we are selling an in-the-money put which may be subject to early exercise which would render the strategy unprofitable. A call bull spread's short position is not in-the-money until the strategy has passed its point of maximum potential profit.

Put bull spreads may be more suited to a trader who has a desire to write puts but is concerned about their ability to manage risk. The put bull spread enables the trader to generate a credit but engage some downside protection.

Bear Spreads

Call Bear Spreads

A call bear spread is created by selling a lower strike price call and buying a higher strike price call—this is the reverse of how we established a call bull spread. As such, the strategy is profitable if the underlying stock declines in value.

To illustrate the construction of a call bear spread, let's use the following values:

ANZ is trading at $18.75

ANZ Oct 1800 call is trading at $1.00

ANZ Oct 1850 call is trading at 85¢

If we sell the Oct 1800 call at $1.00 and buy the Oct 1850 call at 85¢, we have created a call bear spread, because we have sold the lower strike price call. This is a credit transaction. In this example, the credit is 15¢. This represents our maximum potential profit, which would be realised if ANZ dropped sharply and both calls expired worthless. To illustrate this point, consider the range of outcomes in Figure 8.3.

Figure 8.3 *Call Bear Spread Outcomes*

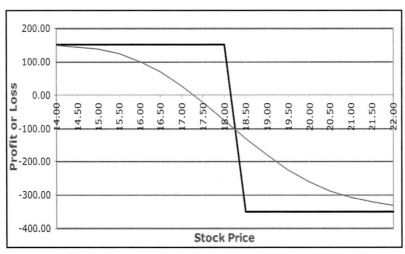

This range of outcomes is exactly the opposite of those possible for a call bull spread. Our maximum profit is limited to our initial credit and the maximum potential loss is 35¢, which is the difference between the two strike prices less the initial credit we received. The breakeven point on this strategy can be defined as being the lower strike price plus the initial credit received, i.e. 1800 + 15 = 1815¢.

Put Bear Spreads

A put bear spread is established by selling a put at a lower strike price and buying a put with a higher strike price. Once again, this is the opposite way to which we would have constructed a bull spread using puts.

As an example, let's use the following prices:

WBC is trading at $14.20

WBC Oct 1400 put is trading at 50¢

WBC Oct 1450 put is trading at 75¢

To construct a put bear spread we would buy the Oct 1450 put and sell the Oct 1400 put. Such a transaction would cost us 25¢. To illustrate what happens at expiry, consider Figure 8.4.

Figure 8.4 *Put Bear Spreads*

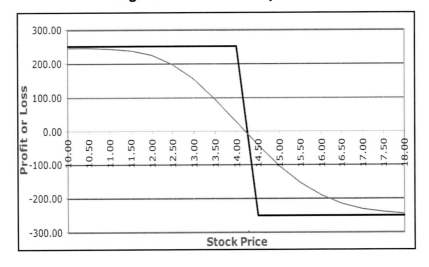

Again our range of outcomes is the reverse of that possible with a put bull spread. Our maximum loss is limited to our initial debit of 25¢ and our maximum profit potential is the difference between the two strike prices minus our initial debit, i.e. 25¢. Our breakeven point is once again defined as the higher strike price minus the initial debit, i.e. $1450 - 25 = 1425$¢.

Just as our optimum way to construct a bull spread was to use calls, the most efficient way to construct a bear spread is to use puts. This is because when constructing a bear spread using calls we are selling an in-the-money call and buying an out-of-the-money call. The result of this is that we are buying more time value than we are selling and this is the opposite to what we would generally like to achieve. The idea of selling calls is to sell those with high time values and let the natural time decay effect quickly reduce the value of the call. There is also the additional consideration that, in selling an in-the-money call, there is always the chance of being exercised before the spread is profitable.

Ratio Spreads

The spread strategies outlined, as well as having exactly the same expiry dates, also had a constant ratio of options bought and sold. For each option bought one was sold; hence, a ratio of 1:1 was established. Such a ratio is not mandatory in constructing a spread.

Consider the following example:

WBC is trading at $14.00

WBC Nov 1450 call is trading at 80¢

WBC Nov 1500 call is trading at 60¢

If we were to buy the 1450 call and sell the 1500 call, we would have constructed a standard bull spread. However, as a variation, if we were to buy one 1450 call and sell two 1500 calls, we would have created a ratio spread. Such a strategy would yield a credit of 40¢.

Ratio spreads are most efficient when established for an initial credit since there is no downside risk. The possible outcomes upon expiry are shown in Figure 8.5 (opposite).

In ratio spreads, there is no downside risk; the risk in the strategy is on the upside where losses can be unlimited.

Since this strategy has a good probability of making a profit with no downside risk, it is one traders should be familiar with. The strategy is very effective when a 1:2 ratio is employed. However, the more aggressive trader may choose a 1:3 ratio to establish a credit position. In fact, this may more often be the case since the efficiency with which the market prices options may make establishing a credit with a 1:2 ratio impossible. However, it is not common to establish a ratio of greater than 1:4 due to the large increase in the upside risk associated with such high ratios.

Figure 8.5 *Ratio Spreads*

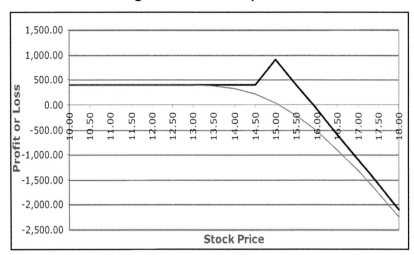

More Advanced Spreads

All the examples of spreads we have dealt with so far have had one element in common: the options from which they were constructed all had the same expiry date. Spreads constructed from options that have the same expiry date are known as vertical spreads. Common expiry dates are not a prerequisite for the creation of a spread. A spread that depends on the sale of one option and the purchase of another option of a different expiry date is known as a calendar spread.

Horizontal Calendar Spread

Suppose the following prices exist in April:

WMC is trading at $10.00

We review the available options and note the following:

WMC May 1000 call is trading at 50¢

WMC Aug 1000 call is trading at 75¢

If we were to sell the May 1000 call and buy the August 1000 call for a net cost of 25¢, we would have created a calendar spread.

Suppose that by May WMC is relatively unchanged in price, then our May 1000 call will expire worthless and our August 1000 call should be worth approximately 50¢. Initially, we have established a spread at a cost of 25¢ and by May our spread is worth 50¢. The August 1000 call can be sold for 50¢ and we would have made a profit of 25¢.

If WMC had dropped sharply, then our risk is limited to our initial debit of 25¢. This is also true if WMC had risen sharply before expiry. Note also that we have protected ourselves against the possibility of exercise by having a long position. If we were to be exercised, we would in turn satisfy delivery requirements by exercising our long position.

The rationale in generating a calendar spread is twofold. Firstly we look to take advantage of the differing rates of time decay experienced by options of differing expiries. Near-dated options have a much greater rate of time decay than distant options.

Secondly, options will often have dislocations in their relative levels of volatility. Consider the following situation:

BHP currently trading at $10.00. Historic volatility is 22%.

BHP July 1050 call trading at 50¢ with an implied volatility of 47%.

BHP September 1050 call trading at 90¢ with an implied volatility of 24%.

Since volatility is mean regressive, we can make the judgement that the July option is overvalued whilst the September option is fairly priced. To take advantage of this we'll sell the July option and buy the September option in the belief that the price of the July option will collapse and the September option will stay reasonably constant. It should be remembered that this is a volatility trade. Direction is irrelevant to the trade; we are seeking only to profit from dislocations in volatility.

Diagonal Calendar Spread

If a trader makes use not only of differing expiry dates but also different strike prices, then a diagonal spread is created.

To illustrate how a variety of spreads can be constructed, assume the following prices exist:

WMC is trading at $10.00

Call Prices

Strike Price	May	EXPIRY August	November
1000	40¢	75¢	95¢
1100	20¢	45¢	55¢

To create a standard bull spread, we would buy the May 1000 call and sell the May 1100 call. To create a calendar spread, we would sell the May 1000 and buy the August 1000. To establish a diagonal calendar bull spread, we would buy the August 1000 and sell the May 1100 call for a debit of 55¢.

Whilst the diagonal calendar spread is more expensive to implement than a standard bull spread, it re-orientates the spread on the downward side. The slightly lower profit potential also means that the probability of total loss is lowered. If the stock falls suddenly, the longer-term call would retain some value because of its greater time to maturity.

The Straddle

Long Straddle

The straddle may be defined as the simultaneous purchase of an equal number of puts and calls that have the same underlying stock, strike price and expiry month. The basic idea in buying a straddle is that the trader perceives that a particular stock will break strongly in a given direction, either up or down, yet the direction of this break is uncertain. Such a situation may occur when a stock approaches a traditional line of resistance—it may either breach this resistance or retreat from it. So for a predetermined outlay, the trader may participate in any movement in the stock.

Like all option buying strategies, the loss is limited to our initial investment and our potential profit is unlimited. As an example, assume that the following prices exist:

RIO is trading at $32.00

RIO July 3200 call is trading at 160¢

RIO July 3200 put is trading at 140¢

If we bought both the July call and the July put, we would own a straddle, the cost of which is 300¢. Figure 8.6 (overleaf) shows the range of possible outcomes.

Notice how there is a direct relationship between our breakeven point and our initial outlay. In this example, our initial outlay was 300¢, therefore, our breakeven range is defined as being the strike price of the option plus or minus our initial debit, i.e. 3200 + 300 = 3500 or 2300 − 300 = 2900. Thus, our breakeven points are $29.00 and $35.00. If RIO is between these points at expiry, we will lose money. If RIO is at exactly $32.00 (an unlikely event) then the possibility exists to lose our total investment.

Straddles are generally only suitable for volatile stocks that have a capacity to move far enough for us to profit during the limited life of our option. As such they fall into the category of option trades known as volatility plays. The future direction of the underlying is unknown but volatility is perceived to be low and expected to rise. From our earlier discussion of volatility it was discovered that volatility is non-directional, so if volatility rises both puts and calls will rise in value.

Figure 8.6   *Long Straddle Payoff Diagram*

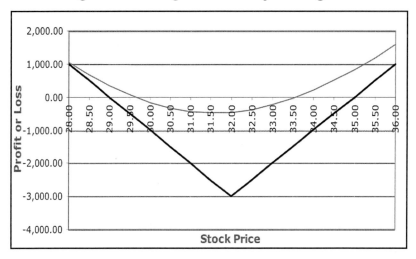

The straddle is best instituted when options are perceived to be undervalued as a function of the underlying volatility assumption.

By now, you have probably realised that any option strategy that can be bought, i.e. is a long position, may be sold or written.

Short Straddle

Just as a bought strategy can be implemented by a trader anticipating a sharp movement, a written straddle is created where such a movement may not be expected. For example, let's assume the following prices:

RIO is trading at $32.00

RIO July 3200 call is trading at 160¢

RIO July 3200 put is trading at 140¢

A straddle can be sold for 300¢; if RIO is between $29.00 and $35.00 at expiry then we will realise a profit. This is shown in Figure 8.7.

Figure 8.7 *Short Straddle Payoff Diagram*

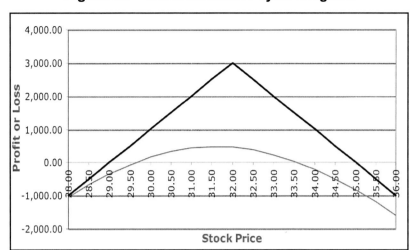

Our maximum profit potential is achieved if RIO finishes at the strike price at expiry and a large potential for losses exists if the stock moves too far in either direction. For this reason, it is imperative that a trader be well versed in the potential risks of such a strategy, such as large price fluctuations and the possibility of being exercised, since one leg of the play is always in-the-money unless the stock remains at the exercise price for the duration of the option. Before putting a sold straddle in place, we should be aware of possible defensive actions.

There are several fall-back positions available if a straddle goes wrong. Firstly, we may simply buy the straddle back. We would never buy back both legs since it is impossible for both sides of the straddle to go wrong simultaneously. This may be an effective strategy if we had to buy our put back since, as has been noted before, put options lose time value very quickly once they are in-the-money. So we may be able to close this leg with minimal losses.

If the market is very bullish and we have to take action to close out the call leg, it may prove to be expensive since the time value of a call option may not shrink by much at all. Hence, buying back a straddle is much more effective in the latter stages of an option's life since their time value decays rapidly.

The written straddle will always present us with a situation of having one leg in-the-money. This presents us with the need to understand how to repair a strategy. This can be done by purchasing an option that caps the liability of the short leg that has gone bad.

For example, if RIO fell sharply then we could buy a 3100 put to cap any potential downside loss. Likewise should RIO break upwards we could purchase a 3300 call to cap the upside loss.

The Written Straddle and Volatility

An option trader who has engaged a written straddle is at greatest risk from an increase in volatility. Traders who use the written straddle should be aware of the role volatility plays in option trading. Remember, should volatility lift, both calls and puts expand in value. You must have a clearly defined exit strategy before engaging this, or any other, option strategy.

Strangles

Long Strangle

In constructing a long strangle the trader is uncertain of market direction but has the perception of a very large move. The trader is also very bullish on volatility. The market needs to make a much larger move than in the case of the straddle in order for the trade to be profitable.

Figure 8.8 *Long Strangle Construction*

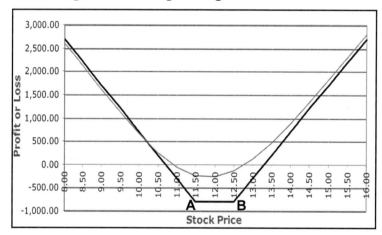

To construct a long strangle, a put is purchased at A (in Figure 8.8) and a call is purchased at B. In this instance both options are out-of-the-money. An alternative construction is to buy a call at A and a put at B. In this instance both legs are in-the-money and the resultant strategy is called a 'long guts'.

For example, if BHP is currently trading at $12.00, a July 1250 call is purchased for 45¢ and a July 1150 put is purchased for 35¢; the combined debit is 80¢. Both positions are out-of-the-money.

The risk is limited to the initial debit, and the reward is potentially unlimited. The low breakeven point is equal to the put strike price minus the debit. The high breakeven point is the call strike price plus the debit.

The wide range over which the trade is unprofitable should dissuade the trader from engaging a long strangle. The strangle requires less capital to establish compared to a straddle but the lower probability of success means a greater chance of traders losing all their money. Any management strategy therefore has to recognise the possibility of the position losing all of its value. The major problems facing a strangle are the relatively low gamma values of the out-of-the-money options, therefore the trade has little bang for bucks. Management must therefore centre on the damage done by stagnation.

Since this trade is sensitive to a lack of movement in the underlying a time stop needs to be initiated to prevent a total loss of capital. Strangles should have some time to run to try and negate theta and to give the price a chance of doing something positive. It should also be remembered that time and volatility are linked. The more time to expiry the greater the impact of any volatility-based move.

Follow-up action is predicated on a move in the underlying either due to direction or volatility. If the move is simply directionally based with no move in the underlying volatility assumptions then one leg of the trade will begin to suffer. It is therefore imperative that action be taken to minimise the damage caused by this leg. This can be done by initiating a stop and letting the profitable leg run or by selling options against the non-performing leg. The capture of premium can offset some of the movement. A volatility move presents a different scenario since it will affect calls and puts equally and may allow the entire strangle to be shut down for a profit. Conversely should volatility drop the entire trade will need to be shut down to prevent a total loss of all premium.

Short Strangle

In constructing the short strangle the view is one of bearish volatility and no major upward directional move by the underlying. A stagnant market where price simply marks time will benefit the strangle.

The risk of this strategy is potentially unlimited. The reward is limited to the initial premium generated. The high side breakeven is equal to the call strike price plus the premium received. The downside breakeven is the put strike price minus the premium received.

The strangle offers the potential for the trader to benefit from a stagnant market and presents a trade that will be profitable over a wide range of prices. However a strong directional move or a lift in volatility will damage a strangle. In the best of all worlds a directional move is preferable to a lift in volatility since a lift in volatility will affect both sides of the strangle whereas the directional move will only damage one side. In comparison to the straddle the strangle collects less premium but is profitable over a wider range of prices due to the fact that both options are out-of-the-money.

To construct a short strangle, a call is sold at B (in Figure 8.9) and a put is sold at A. In this instance both options are out-of-the-money. An alternative construction is to sell a put at A and a call at B; in this instance both options are in-the-money. Such a strategy is referred to as a 'short guts'.

Figure 8.9 *Short Strangle Construction*

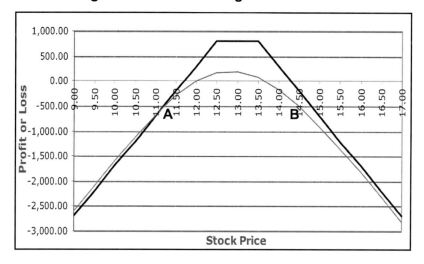

For example, if NCP is trading at $13.00 and we sell a NCP June 1250 put for $0.35 and a NCP June 1350 call for $0.45. This yields a credit of $0.80. This strangle is profitable over the range of NCP prices from $11.70 to $14.30.

The tactics involved in trading a short strangle are identical to those involved in trading the short straddle. The emphasis is once again on the possibility of a strong directional or volatility-based move. The possibility of a directional move is somewhat negated by the often wide range of prices over which the trade can be profitable. The problem lies in a volatility spike since this will damage both sides of the trade. As a result of this we are faced with the need to set a stop on each leg of the trade in the event of a directional move, and a stop on the trade as a unit in case of a volatility spike.

In talking about multi-legged short trades it is necessary for me to return to a train of thought I introduced earlier and that is the need for stops. If you cannot follow a stop do not engage trades with large contingent liabilities. The strangle convinces many traders that there is no need for a stop because of the wide range over which the price of the underlying can move before the trade enters into a loss. However, such a view does not take into account the role of volatility. The possibility of a volatility spike necessitates a stop on the total premium required to buy the position back. A directional move would allow the trader to keep one leg in play whilst shutting down the losing leg either by buying the position back or by putting in place a protective hedge.

9

Warrants

By the end of this chapter you will understand the following:

▲ The basic differences between warrants and ETOs.

▲ The terms relating to the issuing of warrants.

▲ The basic styles of warrants.

The warrant market has changed dramatically since the introduction of warrants over a decade ago. Initially warrants were somewhat of an oddity that suffered from poor support from the issuers, a lack of variety and a lack of interest on behalf of traders who were already being inundated by a variety of failed new product initiatives by both the SFE and the ASX. Many things—most notably the 'tech wreck' of April 2000 and the movement into the market of some very aggressive players such as BNP Paribas and SocGen—have altered the landscape of warrants trading. In November 1997 around 400 million warrants were traded in Australia. In November 2001 this figure was around 1 billion.

What are Warrants?

A warrant can be defined as an option that has been issued by a financial institution such as a merchant bank. In essence warrants are long-dated call or put options. As such they share all the same descriptive elements as options; underlying security, strike price and exercise date. They also share all the same pricing influences and are priced using the same pricing equations. Elements of a warrant's price are also described by the Greeks.

Instead of concentrating upon the similarities between options and warrants I wish to highlight the major differences and how these impact upon the trading of these instruments. The following is a list of the major differences between ETOs and warrants.

Table 9.1 *Differences Between Warrants and Options*

	Warrants	**Options**
Trading system	SEATS	DTF
Clearing system	CHESS	OCH
Issuer	Institution	ASX decides which stocks
Issue terms	Variable	Standardised
Product types	More than 20	Calls/Puts/ Index/LEPO
Lifespan	3 Months to 10 years	Spot, 3,6,9 or 12 months
Liquidity	Guaranteed by issuer	Market Maker
Online trading	Yes	Generally no
Facility to write	No	Yes
Exercise criteria	Dependent upon conversion ratio	1,000 shares

I will now look at some of these individually.

1. Trading System

When traders engage in an options trade they are engaging in a game of hide and seek. Options are quoted on either a continuous basis or on request. If an option is quoted on the basis of request then the trader has to hunt around for a price at which the market maker will deal. This is at times very frustrating and it is an impediment to trading since it leads to

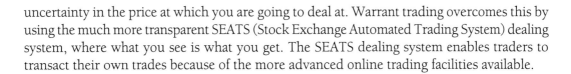

uncertainty in the price at which you are going to deal at. Warrant trading overcomes this by using the much more transparent SEATS (Stock Exchange Automated Trading System) dealing system, where what you see is what you get. The SEATS dealing system enables traders to transact their own trades because of the more advanced online trading facilities available.

2. Clearing System

Transacting business through SEATS means that traders can use a single account to trade warrants and equities without the need to deal with a third party such as the OCH. This ability to trade without involving a third party simplifies the business of trading dramatically.

3. Issuer

One of the great advantages of options is the ability to build trades that take advantage of the features of writing options, such as time decay. This is impossible to do with warrants; the trader is always long the warrant. It is impossible to go short or write a warrant.

When a warrant is brought into existence it is done so by the issuer, who writes it, so this leg of the trade is denied to the warrants trader. The warrant buyer is therefore continually battling the effects of time decay and must constantly take a firm directional view to be profitable. In this area the option trader has a clear advantage because of the greater number of strategies available to engage the market.

The following is a list of the warrant issuers in Australia at the time of writing.

Table 9.2 *Warrant Issuers in Australia*

Issuer letter	Issuer
A	Australia & New Zealand Banking Group Ltd
C	Credit Suisse First Boston Australia Financial Products Ltd
D	Deutsche Bank AG
E	Challenger Equities Ltd
G	SG Australia Ltd
K	Credit Lyonnais Financial Products (Guernsey) Limited
L	Barclays Bank PLC

(cont'd...)

Warrant Issuers in Australia (cont'd)

Issuer letter	Issuer
M	Macquarie Bank Ltd
N	Salomon Smith Barney Australia Pty Ltd
O	Citibank AG
P	BNP Paribas
S	UBS Warburg Ltd
W	Westpac Banking Corporation Ltd
X	Merrill Lynch International and Co. CV
Y	Commonwealth Bank of Australia Ltd
Z	ABN AMRO Australia Ltd

4. Issue Terms

The warrant market is about as organised as a mad woman's breakfast. Warrants are issued with no standardisation of strike price or expiry date. The issuing process is very haphazard. This is a significant disadvantage for warrant traders since it is often difficult to find a warrant that falls within the trading rules they have defined for themselves. Option traders do not suffer from this disadvantage due to the highly structured nature of the options market.

5. Product Type

The warrants market prides itself on having myriad products, however most are almost useless because of a lack of volume. The major type of warrants are equity-based trading warrants. The other more exotic warrants are a long way behind in terms of volume traded. The option market consists of only two viable products, calls and puts.

6. Lifespan

Options work through a strict rotating calendar of three-month cycles with spot months for some stocks. It is unusual to see a large amount of open interest in options that are more than six months from expiry.

Warrants often offer expiry dates of several years. This is a distinct advantage for warrants, since it may serve to insulate the trader from the more dramatic effects of time decay that are the bane of the option buyer's existence. However it must be noted that warrants are not exempt from the effects of time decay; if you buy equivalent warrants and options they will lose time value at the same rate.

7. Liquidity

Both options and warrants require the presence of market makers to ensure an orderly, liquid market. The role of the market maker in both markets is analogous—it is in the execution of that role that the markets differ.

Market makers in the warrant market are highly visible because of the use of the SEATS dealing system. Most market makers provide an open and dynamic presence, and will enable traders to view their pricing parameters by emailing their pricing matrices directly to traders at the start of the trading day. Very aggressive warrant players such as BNP Paribas and SocGen have very active market makers.

The options market does not offer this facility due to the lack of a true trader screen interface and the need to only provide some quotes on a request basis.

8. Exercise Criteria

An option contract gives the contract holder leverage over 1,000 shares. The only situation where this may vary is in the event of a capital reconstruction or issue. At the time of writing such a situation exists in BHP, where, due to the merger with Billiton, a contract covers 1,033 shares.

The warrant market is somewhat different since the leverage over the underlying instrument is determined by the conversion ratio of the individual warrant. The exposure to the underlying instrument can be represented by the following:

Gearing = Price of underlying ÷ Warrants price x Conversion

Gearing represents the exposure to the underlying instrument achieved by the purchase of one warrant.

It is only logical to assume that the percentage price variation for a warrant will be higher than the underlying instrument. This is a function of the leverage (elasticity) of the warrant.

Elasticity is not constant and varies with price, and is given by the following formula:

Elasticity = Gearing ÷ Delta

Warrant Terminology

All warrants are issued with a six-letter ASX code. The individual letters of the code describe some of the main features of the warrant.

The first three letters of the code identify the underlying instrument. For most equity and instalment warrants this will be the same as the ASX code of the underlying company shares.

The fourth letter of the code identifies the type of warrant. This is what these letters stand for:

W Trading style warrants, including equity calls and puts, index calls and puts (including those with barrier levels), currency calls and puts.

I Instalment warrants.

E Endowment warrants.

X Warrants which have significantly different structures to any of the above. These are typically structured-investment style warrants such as capital-protected warrants and capped warrants.

D This is a temporary code assigned to a warrant trading on a deferred settlement basis. Such warrants revert to their original code on the first day of normal trading after deferred settlement period ends.

The fifth letter of the code identifies the warrant issuer. The particular warrants codes are listed earlier in this chapter.

The sixth letter of the code identifies the particular warrant series. The range A to O is reserved for call warrants, while the range P to Z is reserved for put warrants.

Warrant Types

Equity Warrants

These are the easiest warrants to understand. They are issued as either puts or calls over an underlying share. So, like ETOs, they give the holder the right to buy or sell the underlying share at a fixed price throughout the life of the contract

Equity warrants are an excellent tool for traders because they allow a leveraged exposure to the underlying share without the complications that are incurred in other warrants. As such, equity warrants can serve as replacements for similar ETOs.

The table opposite highlights those stocks that attract the most trader interest.

Table 9.3 *Warrant Volume*

Underlying	Volume	% Market
NCP	280,260,370	26.5
BHP	90,132,752	8.5
CBA	85,877,035	8.1
TLS	84,741,373	8.1
NAB	72,693,812	6.9
QAN	53,669,332	5.1
ANZ	45,078,188	4.3
FGL	38,261,108	3.6
BIL	35,355,321	3.3
MIM	20,937,304	2.0

Fractional Warrants

Fractional warrants are similar in most respects to standard equity warrants. However, in the case of a fractional warrant, a number of warrants are required to be exercised per underlying share.

Index Warrants

Index warrants are simply warrants over a given index, such as the S&P 500 or the Nasdaq 100. In this instance the value of the warrant is calculated by applying an appropriate multiplier per point of the index. Such warrants are cash settled.

Basket Warrants

As the name implies such warrants are issued over a group of shares that often carry out similar activities or are members of the same indices. For example a basket warrant may cover a varying ratio of ANZ, CBA, NAB and WBC bank shares. This enables traders to form a view on an industry sector. If I were bullish the banking system, I may buy the basket warrant as a substitute for trading individual equity warrants over each bank. To date basket warrants have not been a great success.

Instalment Warrants

An instalment warrant is similar to a standard equity warrant but with the difference that the warrant holder is entitled to any dividends and franking credits that are paid by the underlying share. Instalment warrants are similar to partly paid shares in that to convert to fully paid ordinary shares a second instalment is due. As such, those who have a long-term view on a given share may trade this view via an instalment warrant. Essentially the fully paid underlying share is on lay-by with the benefit of receiving the full dividend stream on the part payment. Hence, the yield achieved by the long-term trader is higher than if the underlying share had been purchased.

Endowment Warrants

Endowment warrants are an intriguing concept. They are different from standard equity warrants in that they have no fixed exercise date and are European in nature. They work by having what is referred to as an 'outstanding amount' which changes over the life of the warrant. The outstanding amount is determined by the issuer of the warrant at the time of the warrant's creation. In effect, the trader pays a deposit on the warrant of anywhere between 30% and 60%, and over the life of the warrant the outstanding amount is reduced by the payment of dividends from the shares. Once the outstanding amount is paid, the trader becomes the owner of the shares with no more financial commitments. The warrant holder can also elect to pay the outstanding amount during the life of the warrant thereby receiving ownership of the shares before the expiry date.

Sounds too good to be true; merely put a deposit on the shares and the dividends pay off the balance. As one broker trumpets, a solid investment decision—no maintenance equity investment.

Unfortunately the world doesn't work that way. When an endowment warrant is created an interest rate is applied to it which is applied to the balance outstanding. So if you were to purchase CBAWCE, an endowment warrant over CBA, that had a balance outstanding when issued of 6.137%, then you are in a race to see whether the dividends cover the interest payments. The interest rate is defined as the 180-day bank bill swap rate, so this is a floating rate. There is a cut-off date for the endowment warrants after which the issuer can request the warrant holder to pay the outstanding amount or forfeit the warrant.

To place such a vehicle in context you must view the most negative of scenarios. Assume you have purchased one of these warrants with the view to having the maturity coincide with your retirement. Your plan is based on the premise that the warrant has, say, ten years to maturity and that is approximately the length of time until you retire. It is your thought that ten years would be more than sufficient for the dividend stream to pay off the outstanding amount. However, let's assume that we encounter a five-year period of high interest rates (such periods occur with regularity) and the interest rate on your warrant accelerates to 15%. Under such a scenario, the dividend stream cannot keep pace with the outstanding amount and you arrive at retirement facing the prospect of having to pay a substantial outstanding amount.

Risks in Warrant Trading

Just as there are risks in trading ETOs there are also risks in trading warrants. If you cannot trade shares successfully, then you will simply transfer your lack of success to trading warrants.

The prime risk faced by a warrant trader is that the issuer may go belly up and not meet its obligations in terms of delivery. The purchase of a warrant establishes a contract between you and the issuer. If the issuer defaults on its obligations then it is up to you to seek redress. It is important to note that the ASX, whilst being the platform for warrant trading, does not act as a guarantor for the issuer, just as it does not act as guarantor for any of the vehicles listed on the stock exchange.

As I mentioned earlier, one of my initial concerns about warrants is the lack of liquidity in the market. This problem has to a degree been alleviated by investor familiarity with warrants and by the entrance of more dynamic issuers. However, this is no guarantee that you will get what you deem to be a fair price in a thin market. The issuer is required to stand in the market. However, in the absence of anybody else they will stand in the market at a price that is favourable to them.

Normal market risks apply in warrant trading just as they do in ETOs. Warrants are just another financial tool and they respond to the vagaries of the market as does every other listed security. They will not guarantee you a profit despite what your broker has told you. Make an imprudent trading decision with warrants and you will lose money just as you would trading options or shares. The age-old rule of buyer beware applies.

Appendix –
Option Expiry

The expiry date of an option is fixed according to one of the following cycles:

January, April, July, October

ANZ, AXA, CCL, CPU, DVT, ERG, FBG, FXJ, GMF, MIM, NAB, OSH, PPX, QRL, SGB, TAH, WBC

February, May, August, November

AMC, AM1, BLD, CML, LHG, LLC, MAY, MBL, NCM, NCP, NC1, NDY, ORG, ORI, PAS, PDP, QAN, SEV, STO, TEN, TQL

March, June, September, December

AGL, AMP, BHP, BIL, CSR, CWO, DJS, NRM, PBL, RIO, SRP, TAB, TLS, WMC, WOW, WPL, XPI, XJO

In addition to this quarterly cycle the following stocks also have 'spot months'. These options are listed 10 business days before the expiry of the nearest month.

AMP, CBA, CML, NCM, QAN, SEV, STO, TEN, TLS, WPL

In addition to this the following stocks have a rolling three-month spot expiry.

AMP, ANZ, BHP, CBA, CWO, FBG, MIM, NAB, NCP, NDY, PDP, RIO, TLS, WBC, WMC

Glossary

American option

An American style option allows the holder of the contract to exercise at any time during the life of the contract up to and including the day of expiry. All exchange traded options traded in Australia are American in style.

Arbitrage

Arbitrage is used by professional investors to take advantage of price anomalies that may occur between two markets. For example if an arbitrageur decides that a given option is overpriced relative to its underlying stock they may choose to buy the stock and sell the option.

At-the-money

An option is said to be at-the-money when its exercise price is equal to the current market price of the underlying security. For example a BHP 850 call would be at-the-money when BHP was trading at $8.50. Similarly a BHP 850 put would be at-the-money also.

Average down

In my opinion, to buy more of a security the price of which has declined is a recipe for disaster. This is akin to hanging onto the deck of the Titanic as it went down.

Basket warrant

A warrant that has been issued over a basket of shares. For example an institution may issue a warrant over the four major banks or a select group of resource stocks.

Bear/bearish

A bear is someone with a negative expectation of the market or a given stock. If I bought ANZ puts I would be bearish ANZ, since I would be expecting a fall in price.

Bear spread

Creating a spread involves the simultaneous writing of an option with a lower strike price whilst purchasing an option with a higher strike price, usually with the same expiry date. For example if I were to sell the BHP 850 call and buy the 900 call I would have created a call bear spread. Such a strategy would have only a limited profit potential.

Beta

The degree to which a stock moves relative to the market. For example if a stock has a beta of 1.50 then for a given move in the market this stock will move an additional 50%.

Board broker

The board broker is an employee of the OCH who executes public limit orders on behalf of various clearing members.

Break even point

The price at which a trade neither makes nor loses money.

Bull/bullish

Someone who is a bull has an expectation that the market will rise.

Bull spread

Constructing a bull spread involves buying a lower strike price option at the same time as selling an option with a higher strike price.

Buy and write

A buy and write, which is sometimes referred to as a scrip-covered write, involves simultaneously purchasing shares and then selling a number of calls that are equivalent to the number of shares that have been purchased. Buy and writes enable traders to potentially increase the rate of return they achieve by holding shares while at the same time providing a limited degree of downside protection.

Calendar spread

Constructing a calendar spread involves writing a near-month option and buying a far-month option at the same strike price.

Call option

A call option gives the holder the right but not the obligation to buy a fixed number of shares at a given price at any date up to a fixed expiry date.

Called away

Being called away refers to the process when the writer of a call option is required to sell the underlying security to a call option buyer as part of fulfilling their obligations. Being called away is something the naked option writer fears.

Carrying cost

The interest expense involved in purchasing an options position.

Cash covered option

A written option that has had cash lodged as security with the OCH. Also referred to as a naked options position since there is no underlying security to support the position in the event of the stock being called away.

Class deposit

The initial value of cash or collateral that is required to be paid by a naked option writer to the OCH. The level of deposit required is set by the OCH and varies from share to share.

Clearing member

A member organisation of the ASX which has been admitted as a clearing member of the OCH. A clearing member is generally the broker you deal through, and is entitled to trade on the floor of the OCH on behalf of clients.

Closing call prices

Also known as CCPs, these are the daily closing buy and sell prices for puts and calls. CCPs are used to establish daily margin requirements.

Closing purchase

Any trade that liquidates a trader's written option position. For example if I had written CBA 1000 calls then the transaction that buys these calls back is referred to as a closing purchase.

Closing sale

Any trade that liquidates a trader's bought position. For example if I had BHP 1800 puts and I sold them then this would be a closing sale.

Collar

A strategy that requires a trader to simultaneously write a put (call) and buy a call (put) in the same security but with different exercise prices. The aim of the strategy is to establish an upper and lower limit within which the strategy will generate a profit. You effectively put a collar around the stock.

Collateral cover

A value the OCH assigns to any security be it shares, bank guarantees or any other instrument that is lodged with the OCH as security for margins and deposits.

Combination

Any trade that involves simultaneous buying and selling of puts and calls with different exercise prices and/or expiry dates.

Contingent order

An order where one leg of a transaction is dependent upon another. For example if I were establishing a bull spread I might make the short leg of the trade contingent upon getting the long leg in place.

Cum

Latin word meaning with. Cum bonus, cum rights, cum dividend are all conditions that attach to the underlying security.

Delivery

The act of fulfilling your obligations under the terms of the option contract that you have incurred as the writer of that option. For example if I have written BHP 900 calls and I am required to deliver then I must sell to the option buyer BHP at $9.

Delta

The degree to which an option price will move given a movement in the underlying security. An option with a delta of 0.5 will move half a cent for every full cent movement in the underlying stock. Deeply out-of-the-money calls have a delta approximating zero, at-the-money calls 0.5 and deeply in-the-money calls have a delta approximating 1.

Delta spread

A spread that is established as neutral position using the deltas of the options involved.

Diagonal spread

A strategy that requires a trader to write one option and take another option. Each option will have the same underlying security but will have different exercise prices and expiry dates.

Discount

An option is said to be trading at a discount when it is trading for less than its intrinsic value.

Downside protection

Insurance against any downward move in the underlying stock. Buying puts against physical stock or buying and writing confer downside protection.

Early exercise

Not something a naked option writer looks forward to. Early exercise refers to any option that is exercised prior to the expiry date.

Endowment warrant

A warrant where the outstanding balance is paid for by the accumulation of dividends from the underlying share.

ETO

Exchange traded option.

European option

An option contract that only allows exercise on the date of expiry.

Exercise

To invoke the right that is attached to an option contract. For example if I own a call option I have the right to buy the underlying stock at a given price. If I choose to take up the underlying stock I have exercised my right under the terms of the contract.

Exercise limit

The number of options that may be exercised over a given security in any given period. Exercise limits are seen in action during a takeover. They are designed to prevent traders from gaining a dominant position in the shares of a given company via the options market.

Exercise notice

Not something the naked option writer wants to see. An exercise notice is issued by the OCH and instructs an option writer to, in the case of a call writer, deliver stock at the exercise price specified; or for a put writer to take delivery of the stock at the specified exercise price.

Exercise price

The strike price of an option. It is the price at which an option may be exercised.

Expiration

The date at which all unexercised options lapse.

Expiration cycle

The time intervals between the option series. Whilst many options have what are termed spot months, the typical option has a three-month cycle based upon one of the following cycles:

January/April/July/October

February/March/August/November

March/June/September/December.

Expiry month

The month in which an option expires.

Fair value

The theoretical price of an option as defined according to a mathematical pricing model. Because each model has a variety of variables differing fair values will be obtained by a range of models. A cynic would argue that fair value can be defined as any price that you, the trader, don't pay.

Far month

The option series with the longest time to expiry.

Good until cancelled

A fairly rare order in options markets. If I were to give my broker an order to buy BHP July 900 calls at 95¢ and add the proviso that the order was good till cancelled my broker would reinstate the order at the beginning of each day. Options orders are generally day-only due to the inherent volatility of the market.

Hedge

Any strategy or trade that reduces a trader's risk to adverse price movements.

Historical volatility

A measure of how much a share price has moved over a given period of time.

Holder

Any purchaser of an options contract.

Implied volatility

The potential for the price of the underlying security to move based upon the current option premium. When an option price is calculated using a mathematical model a number of variables are input into the equation. These variables include time to expiry, the price of the underlying share, dividends and the current level of interest rates and volatility. If the current option price and the theoretical price are in agreement then it can be assumed that the volatility used in the equation is correct. By manipulating the equation it is possible to obtain a figure for the volatility of the underlying share. The volatility is said to be implied since it was derived from the current price of the option.

In-the-money

When the exercise price of a call (put) is below (above) the current market value of the underlying security. For example if BHP were trading at $9.00 then an 850 call would be said to be in-the-money. A put would be in-the-money only if its strike price were above $9.00, e.g. 950.

Index option

An option over a share index.

Index warrant

A warrant over a particular share index.

Initial deposit

Cash that has been lodged with a clearing member (your broker) by any trader who has written a naked option or cash covered position.

Intrinsic value

In-the-money options are said to possess intrinsic value. It is the difference between the exercise price of the option and the price of the underlying security. For example if ANZ were at $19.10 then an ANZ 1850 call which was trading at 70¢ would be said to have an intrinsic value of 60¢ (1910 – 1850 = 60) and a time value of 10¢ (70 – 60 = 10¢).

Legging it in

A mechanism whereby option trades involving many variables such as complex spreads are assembled one leg at a time instead of simultaneously. It is possible that in doing so you expose yourself to the risk that the market may move suddenly between the establishment of each leg thereby destroying the underlying reason for the strategy. In terms of risk it is analogous to straddling an electric fence as opposed to hurdling it.

LEPO

Low exercise price option.

Liquidity

The level of trade in a given option. Many option stocks are notoriously illiquid making them extremely difficult to trade.

Long position

Any trader who has bought options is said to be long either the market or the underlying security.

Long term options

Options with expiry dates of two and three years.

Margin

When you write an options position there are certain market conditions that will impact adversely upon your position. If you are a call writer a lift in the market will damage your position. Likewise if you are put writer a fall in the market will degrade your equity. To compensate for these fluctuations the OCH calculates a daily margin based upon the movement of your option. The purpose of a margin is to protect your clearing member and by extension the OCH against any potential losses that may be incurred by a movement against your position.

Mark to the market

The process by which margins are calculated using the closing call prices.

Market maker

See registered trader.

Market order

An instruction to your broker to buy or sell at the prevailing market price. Something to be wary of.

Naked option

A position where the writer of an option does not own the underlying security. By definition all written puts are naked.

Neutral

A situation where you expect the market to remain fairly constant. You are neither bullish nor bearish. An example of a neutral strategy would be a written straddle.

Neutral price hedge

A strategy constructed so that any movement in the value of the long position is compensated for by an equal upward movement in the value of the short position. For example if I owned shares against which I had bought the appropriate number of puts, any downward move in the value of the shares is compensated for by a move up in the value of the puts.

Offsets

A reduction in margin payments that are available to option traders as a result of holding positions of the same class.

Open interest

A measure of liquidity. It defines the number of outstanding contracts in a given option series.

Opening purchase

Any transaction in which a trader becomes the buyer or taker of an option.

Opening sale

Any transaction in which the trader becomes the writer of an option.

Options Clearing House (OCH)

The OCH is the overseer of the options market. It acts as the registrar of the market in that it guarantees the performance of all contracts, monitors and imposes margins, and reviews the financial situation of member firms. The OCH plays a prime role in generating confidence in the efficacy and professionalism of the market.

Out-of-the-money

A call option with a strike price greater than the price of the underlying security or a put option with a strike price lower than the price of the underlying security. It is therefore obvious that an out-of-the-money option has no intrinsic value, its premium is therefore a reflection of purely time value.

Overvalued

A catch-all term used to describe anything that is trading at a higher than expected value.

Parity

Parity is achieved when an option is trading at intrinsic value only.

Pay-off diagrams

The funny little charts that litter this book. Typically they are used to give a visual interpretation of the range of outcomes for various strategies.

Position limit

The maximum number of options contracts that may be held by one trader.

Premium

Another word for the price of an option.

Price spread

Any option strategy that uses options of the same expiry dates but with different exercise prices.

Profit range

The prime consideration for any trader. It is the range of prices within which an options strategy will make a profit.

Put option

An options contract that gives the buyer the right but not the obligation to sell a fixed number of shares at a given price on or before an expiry date.

Random selection

The method by which the OCH assigns exercise notices.

Ratio strategy

Any strategy that involves unequal numbers of options.

Registered Traders (RTs)

I have heard many definitions of RTs over the years, most are unprintable. Because options are a wasting asset there is the possibility that as expiry nears liquidity in a given options series will dry up. To counter this problem the OCH appoints RTs who are obliged to make a market in their appointed stock. RTs have to provide a bid and offer for a minimum number of contracts thereby ensuring liquidity. That's the theory.

Return if exercised

The amount of profit that a scrip covered writer may expect if the option they have written is exercised.

Return if unchanged

The profit that may be expected if the price of an underlying security does not alter before expiry.

Roll down

The closing out of all options positions in a given series and at the same time opening new positions in the same series but at a lower strike price.

Roll up

The closing out of all options positions in a given series and at the same time opening new positions in the same series but with a higher strike price.

Rolling

Closing of any option position in a given series and at the same time opening a new position in the same option series.

Scrip-covered option

An option in which the writer owns the underlying security.

Series of options

Options with the same characteristics, i.e. strike price and expiry date.

Short selling

The strategy of selling an instrument that you do not already own in the belief that the price will fall and the security can be bought back at a lower price. For example if I were to short sell ANZ at $19.00 my belief would be that I could buy it back at below $19.00.

Spot options

Options which have a life span of one month from the time of listing.

Spread

Any strategy that involves the simultaneous buying and selling of options.

Spread orders

Requires that buy and sell orders be executed simultaneously. You know your broker has a good operator if he can pull this off without too much drama.

Straddle

A strategy that requires the simultaneous buying or selling of equal numbers of puts and calls with the same expiry date and strike price.

Strangle

A strategy that requires the buying or writing of two options, a put and a call. The strategy requires that the options used must be of the same expiry date but with different strike prices. The object of a strangle is to squeeze a stock between two strike prices.

Strike price

See exercise price.

Taker

Another word for the buyer of an option.

Theoretical value

See fair value.

Time value

The amount by which an option's value exceeds its intrinsic value.

Uncovered option

See naked option.

Undervalued

When an option is trading at a value lower than the theoretical price.

Volatility

The degree to which the price of an underlying security could reasonably be expected to move.

Warrant

An option that has been issued by a third party and is traded on the ASX.

Writer

The seller of an option.

Index

www.artoftrading.com.au

Consultancy Services

The Art of Trading Pty Ltd holds seminars and training sessions on a regular basis.

No matter what your level of experience, there will be a trading tool to improve your trading results at www.artoftrading.com.au. The products and services provided include:

▶ A complete online shop

▶ Free products to download, such as a variety of trading games and money management tools

▶ A collection of articles

▶ Access to The Trading Game Forum

▶ An Option Strategy Guide pdf, an Option Trader Home Study Course and an Option Strategies Poster.

For more information, visit: www.artoftrading.com.au

Art of Trading Pty Ltd
PO Box 1171
Caulfield North 3161

info@artoftrading.com.au

Option Trader
Home Study Course
Special Offer

The Option Trader Home Study Course download will complement the information presented in this book. It assumes an intermediate understanding of option trading strategies and technical analysis. It will take you a step further in developing your analytical and trading skills. You will also receive one year of personal support and mentoring via **The Trading Game Forum (www.tradinggame.com.au)**. You will be able to ask questions directly of Chris Tate and Louise Bedford (author of *The Secret of Writing Options*).

Clip out this coupon, print all details clearly, tick where appropriate, sign, date and post to: The Art of Trading Pty Ltd, PO Box 1171, Caulfield North, Vic. 3161. *Only original forms will be accepted, and your email address must be capable of accepting a 2mb pdf file.*

- -

Option Trader Home Study Course

☐   YES I wish to receive The Option Trader Home Study Course at the discounted price of $475 (usual price $550).

Please charge my credit card:

☐ Visa   ☐ Mastercard   ☐ Bankcard

Card No.:_____ Expiry Date: _____

Full Name:_____

Mailing Address: _____

Email Address: _____

Daytime Phone No.:_____

Signature:_____

Also by Christopher Tate...

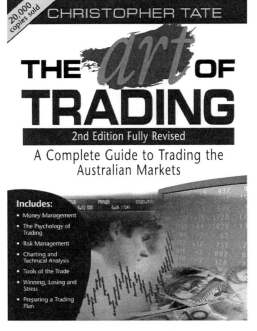

20,000 copies sold

CHRISTOPHER TATE

THE *art* OF
TRADING
2nd Edition Fully Revised
A Complete Guide to Trading the
Australian Markets

Includes:
- Money Management
- The Psychology of Trading
- Risk Management
- Charting and Technical Analysis
- Tools of the Trade
- Winning, Losing and Stress
- Preparing a Trading Plan

The Art of
Trading
2nd Edition

With 20,000 copies sold *The Art of Trading* is firmly established as one of the leading books on trading the financial markets published in Australia.

What sort of job is private trading? It could be described as a craft. There is definitely a high level of skill involved, and trading also requires a certain way of thinking. But above all Chris Tate believes that trading is an art—a combination of skill, talent, imagination, discipline and, possibly, innate ability.

One of the reasons for the enormous success of Chris Tate as a trader, speaker and writer on the subject is that he does not follow the crowd. He opens this book with discussion on the psychology of trading and risk and money management, which is not what you might traditionally expect. The explanation of chart patterns and indicators comes towards the end.

...Available from all good bookshops.

Also by Christopher Tate...

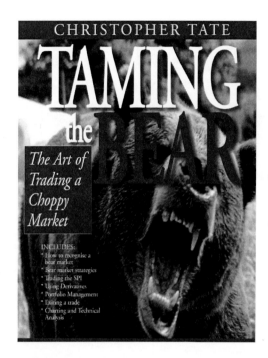

Taming
the Bear

A bear market may last for a week, a month or even a few years, but it can take only a day, an hour or even a few minutes for the value of an investment portfolio to be slashed to half its former value. Of course, not even the experts can accurately forecast what the markets will do. However, there are signs that can indicate a bear market is approaching and, if recognised, give prudent investors time to take steps to safeguard their portfolios.

The first part of this book describes how to recognise the signals that can precede a bear market, and how to watch the various indices for sell signals. The second part deals with methods to help both investors and traders survive by understanding what changes in volume represent, when to use a moving average and how to stay ahead of the pack.

...Available from all good bookshops.

Printed in Australia
13 Dec 2024
LP038636